ULFAZ UDWIYEH,

OR THE

MATERIA MEDICA

ULFAZ UDWIYEH,

OR THE

MATERIA MEDICA

IN THE

Arabic, Persian, and Hindevy Languages

COMPILED BY

NOUREDDEEN MOHAMMED ABDULLAH SHIRAZY

TRANSLATED BY
FRANCIS GLADWIN

GYAN

Published by

GYAN

Gyan Publishing House
5, Ansari Road
Daryaganj, New Delhi-110002
Phone: 011-47034999, 9811692060
E-mail: books@gyanbooks.com

Distribution Network
gyanbooks.com
India, USA, Canada, UK, Australia, France

ISBN: 978-81-212-9110-1 (PB)
First Published, 1793

2nd Impression 2023

Printed at: Gyan Press, Delhi.

ULFAZ UDWIYEH, OR THE MATERIA MEDICA
COMPILER: NOUREDDEEN MOHAMMED ABDULLAH SHIRAZY, TRANSLATOR: FRANCIS GLADWIN

الفاظ ادويه

تصنيف نور الدين محمد عبد الله شيرازي

ULFÁZ UDWIYEH,

OR THE

MATERIA MEDICA,

IN THE

Arabic, Persian, and Hindevy Languages.

COMPILED BY

NOUREDDEEN MOHAMMED ABDULLAH SHIRÁZY,

PHYSICIAN TO THE EMPEROR SHÁHJEHÁN.

WITH AN ENGLISH TRANSLATION,
BY
FRANCIS GLADWIN.

CALCUTTA:

PRINTED AT THE CHRONICLE PRESS.

MDCCXCIII.

JOHN LAI·RD, Esq.

PRESIDENT, AND MEMBERS

OF THE HOSPITAL BOARD,

FORT WILLIAM.

GENTLEMEN,

THE following Work being publiſhed at your Recommendation, for the uſe of the Honourable Company, I beg leave to place it under your immediate Protection.

I HAVE THE HONOUR TO BE,

GENTLEMEN,

YOUR MOST OBEDIENT,

HUMBLE SERVANT,

FRANCIS GLADWIN.

CALCUTTA,
SEPTEMBER 10, 1793.

INTRODUCTION.

OF MEDICINES IN GENERAL.

THE Arabian physicians, in deſcribing the quality or power of medicines, make uſe of four degrees.

The FIRST DEGREE, is that whoſe quality makes imperceptible impreſſion; ſuch as thoſe that are hot, or thoſe that are cold, &c. but which are not felt, unleſs they are reiterated. The SECOND DEGREE, is that which is more powerful than the former, but not ſo much as to occaſion any viſible injury. The THIRD DEGREE is that whoſe impreſſion is eſſentially hurtful, but not ſo as to deſtroy. The FOURTH DEGREE, is that whoſe nature is ſuch that it either kills or materially injures; and this is the property of poiſonous medicines.

NAMES.		QUALITIES. HOT.	COLD.	DRY.	MOIST.
		DEGREES.			
افسنتين	*ÁFSUNTEEN* Wormwood	1	0	3	0
بابونه	*Bá-booneh* Camomile flowers	1	0	1	0
تمر	*Temr* Date	1	0	0	0
تخم كتان	*Tokhem kut-án* Linſeed	1	0	0	0
حمص	*Himmis* A ſpecies of vetch	1	0	3	1
رمان	*Rum-mán* Pomegranate	1	0	0	0
حلزون	*Hulzoon* Snail	1	0	0	0
شاهتره	*Sháhtereh* Fumitory	1	0	2	0
صبر	*Syb-ir* Aloes	1	0	3	0
لوف	*Loof* Dragonwort	1	0	0	0
لاذن	*Làdun* Labdanum	1	0	0	0

	NAMES.	QUALITIES.			
		HOT.	COLD.	DRY.	MOIST.
		DEGREES.			
اسغاقس	*Iſkà-kiſs* A ſpecies of melilot	2	o	o	o
اصل الغرب	*Aſſul ul ghur-eb* Root of the mountain pine	2	o	o	o
اصل المازريون	*Aſſul ul màzreeyoon* Mezereon root	2	o	3	o
سپيد وسياه بادروج	*Sepeid wu ſeyàh badroj*, Two ſpecies of ſweet baſil	2	o	o	o
برنجاسف	*Bir-en-jà-ſif* Mugwort	2	o	o	o
بلسان	*Bulſàn* The balſam tree	2	o	2	o
بزر الانجره	*Buz-ir-ul unjereh* Nettle ſeed, alſo the leaves, an infuſion of	2	o	o	o
جندبيدستر	*Joondbeyduſter* Caſtor	2	o	2	o
حلبه	*Hulbeh* Fenugreek	2	o	o	o
دبق	*Dibk* A ſmall grain which is very viſcous	2	o	o	o
دردي عصاره زيتون	*Doordee aſſàreh zietoon* Dregs of olive oil	2	o	3	o
زراوند طويل ومدحرج	*Zeràwund teweel wu Moodehrej* Birthwort, long, and round	2	o	2	o
زعفران	*Zà-fràn* Saffron	2	o	o	o
شبت	*Shib-it* Fennel	2	o	o	o
عسل	*Aſſul* Honey	2	o	2	o
عنصل	*Unſul* Squill	2	o	o	o

قثاء الحمار

	NAMES	QUALITIES. HOT.	COLD.	DRY.	MOIST.
		DEGREES.			
قثاءالحمار	*Kissa-ul-hymár* Wild cucumber	2	0	0	0
فراسيون	*Frá-seé-yoon* Euphrasia, eyebright	2	0	0	0
قشورشجرة الحية	*Kushoor, shijuret ul hyut* Gentian bark	2	0	0	0
قصب الزريره	*Kusseb us ze-ree-ráh* Wormwood plant.	2	0	2	0
كبريت	*Kib-reet* Sulphur	2	0	0	0
كرفس	*Kerefs* Parsley	2	0	0	0
كمافيطوس	*Kum-á-fee-toos* Ground pine	2	0	3	0
كندر	*Koondir* Frankincense, of which there are three kinds	2	0	1	0
مصطكي	*Moos-te-ká* Mastich	2	0	2	0
ملح	*Mil-h* Culinary salt	2	0	0	0
ميعه	*Mee-áh* Storax	2	0	0	0
وسخ الكوارير	*Wusk-ul-ke-wá-reer* Fresh bees' wax	2	0	0	0
انيسون	*Ánee-soon* Aniseed	3	0	3	0
اسارون	*Assá-roon* Asarabaca	3	0	3	0
افتيمون	*Áfteemoon* Dodder of thyme	3	0	3	0
فنجنكشت	*Funj-ungoosht* Agnus castus, or the chaste tree, it's leaves and seed	3	0	3	0
پودنهجبلي	*Pode-neh Je-be-lee* Wild mint	3	0	0	0
ترب	*Toorb* Radish, the root, and also the leaves	3	0	2	0
جاوشير	*Já-we-sheer* Gum opopanax	2	0	2	0

	NAMES.	QUALITIES. HOT.	COLD.	DRY.	MOIST.
		DEGREES.			
حاشا	*Há-ſhá* thyme	3	0	3	0
حرمل	*Hírmul* Seed of wild rue	3	0	0	0
حماما	*He-má-má* True amomum	3	0	0	0
خربقين	*Khir-be-kine* The two hellebores	3	0	0	0
سداب	*Sood-áb* Rue	3	0	3	0
سرو	*Sir-ou* The cypreſs tree	3	0	4	0
سكبينج	*Suck-bee-nej* Gum ſagapenum	3	0	0	0
سليخه	*Se-lee-kheh* Caſſia lignea	3	0	3	0
شب محرق	*Shebb-moh-ruck* Burnt alum	3	0	3	0
شراب كهنه	*She-ràb kohneh* Old wine	3	0	3	0
شعر محرق	*Sheir moh-ruck* Burnt hair	3	0	3	0
شيح ارمني محرق	*Sheeh urmenee mohruck* A ſpecies of wormſeed burnt	3	0	3	0
صوف محرق	*Soof moh-ruck* Burnt wool	3	0	0	0
غار	*Ghár* Laurel	3	0	3	0
فودنج نهري	*Fode-nej neh-ree* Water mint	3	0	3	0
قشور قصب محرق	*Kuſhoor kuſſeh moh-ruck* Burnt bark of the reed	3	0	3	0
قنه	*Koon-neh* Galbanum	3	0	0	0
كرويا	*Koor-weeya* Caraway ſeed	3	0	3	0
كاشم	*Káſhim* Lovage	3	0	0	0

كرفس بري

	NAMES.	QUALITIES. HOT.	COLD.	DRY.	MOIST.
		DEGREES.			
كرفس بري	*Ke-refs bir-ree* Wild parſley	3	0	0	0
كمادريوس	*Ke-má-der-yoos* Germander	3	0	3	0
مرماحوز	*Mir-má-booz* An odoriferous plant	3	0	0	0
مرزنجوش	*Mir-zun-jooſh* Marjoram	3	0	3	0
نانخواه	*Nán-khàwb* Biſhop's weed, ammi	3	0	0	0
نعناع	*Ná-ná-á* A ſpecies of mint, very pungent	3	0	0	0
ينبوت	*Yum-boot* An Arabian pulſe	3	0	3	0
وج	*Wuj* ſweet flag	3	0	3	0
يتوعات	*Ye-too-áát* General name for milky plants	3	0	0	0
بصل	*Be-ſel* Onion	4	0	0	0
ثوم	*Soom* Garlic	4	0	4	0
زبد البحر	*Ze-bed'ul behr* Foam of the ſea, that adheres to rocks	4	0	0	0
سداب بري	*Soo-dáb bir-ree* Wild rue	4	0	0	0
فربيون	*Fir-be-yoon* Euphorbium	4	0	0	0
قسط	*Kouſt* Coſtus	4	0	0	0
قطران	*Kit-rán* Pitch	4	0	4	0
كراث	*Koor-ráſs* Leek	4	0	4	0
اصل السوس	*Uſſu'lus' ſoos* Liquorice root	0	1	1	0
اقاقيا ناشسته	*A'ka-kyá ná ſhooſ-teh* Acacia not waſhed, or prepared	0	1	3	0
برگ قصب	*Birg kuſſeb* Leaves of the reed	0	0	0	0
برادهٔ نحاس	*Boo-ra-deh no-báſs* Copper filings	0	0	0	0

برگ بنفشه

	NAMES.	QUALITIES. HOT.	COLD.	DRY.	MOIST.
		DEGREES.			
برک بنفشه	*Birg be-nuf-ſheb* Violet leaves	0	1	0	0
بسفایج	*Buſs-fá-yej* Polypody	0	1	3	0
بلوط	*Bu-loot* Acorn	0	1	3	0
ثمرة العليق	*Sumrétul u-leik* Blackberry	0	1	0	0
ثيل	*Seel* Couch graſs	0	1	0	0
جاورس	*Ja-wirſs* A ſpecies of millet	0	1	0	0
جبن رطب	*Jubn-retb* New cheeſe	0	1	0	0
خشخاش	*Khuſh-kháſh* Poppy	0	1	0	0
دلب	*Doolb* The plane tree	0	1	0	0
دهن الورد	*Duhn ul wurd* Oil of roſes	0	1	0	1
زجاج	*Zoojáj* Glaſs	0	1	0	0
زنجفر	*Zunjefr* Cinnabar, native	0	1	0	0
سرمق	*Sir-muck* Stinking orach	0	1	0	2
شجرة النبق	*Shejrut'n-nubk* The lote tree	0	1	0	0
عجم الزبيب	*Ujm uz zebeeb* Grape ſtones	0	1	2	0
کمثري	*Koommuſrá* Pear	0	1	1	0
ماميثا	*Má-my-ſá* The expreſſed juice of a ſpecies of poppy	0	1	0	0
نشاسته	*Na-ſháſ-teh* Starch	0	1	0	0
هندبا	*Hindbá* Endive	0	1	0	0
اقاقيا مغسول	*Aká-ky-á mugh-ſoil* Waſhed (prepared) acacia	0	2	0	0
اطراف وبرک زيتون	*Utráf wu berg zietoon* Leaves and branches of the olive tree	0	2	3	0

هليون

	NAMES.	QUALITIES. HOT.	COLD.	DRY.	MOIST.
		DEGREES.			
هليون	*Hil-yoon* Aſparagus	0	2	0	0
بطيخ	*Beteek* Muſk melon	0	2	0	2
يمانيه	*Yema-nee-a* A ſpecies of chicory, growing in marſhy places	0	2	0	2
بزرقطونا	*Buz-ir ke-too-na* Fleawort ſeed	0	2	0	0
جمار	*Jummár* Pith of the date tree	0	2	0	0
خوخ	*Khoakh* Peach	0	2	0	1
خيار	*Khyár* Cucumber	0	2	0	1
رصاص	*Réſſáſs* Tin	0	2	0	0
زيتون خام	*Zietoon khám* Unripe olives	0	2	0	0
سماق	*Sumák* Sumach	0	2	0	0
تخم اترج	*Tokhum ootruj* Citron ſeed	0	2	0	0
طحلب	*Tuh-leb* Water moſs	0	2	0	1
عفص	*Uf-iſs* Gall apple, unripe	0	2	0	0
كدو	*Ké-doo* A large kind of cucumber, or gourd, with a thin rind	0	2	0	0
لسان الحمل	*Leſſán ul huml* Narrow-leav'd plantain, or ribwort	0	2	4	0
ماش	*Máſh* A ſmall kind of grain	0	2	0	0
مغره	*Moghreh* Red earth	0	2	0	0
كلم	*Ke-lum* Cabbage	0	2	2	0
برشيان دارو	*Bir-ſhe-an-da-roo* A pot-herb of a red colour	0	2	0	0
بقلة الحمقا	*Bucklet 'l humeká* Purſlain	0	2	0	2

جلنار

	NAMES.	QUALITIES.			
		HOT.	COLD.	DRY.	MOIST.
		DEGREES.			
جلنار	*Joolnar* Wild roſe	0	3	3	0
حب العليق خام	*Hub ul uleik kham* Unripe blackberries	0	3	3	0
حماض الاترج	*Hum-áz-ul ooturj* Citron juice	0	3	0	0
حي العالم	*Hy-ul-áálum* Houſe-leek	0	3	1	0
خشخاش سياه	*Khuſh-káſh ſee-áh* Black poppy	0	3	0	0
عصي الراعي	*Aſyr'rá-ey* A pot-herb of a red colour	0	3	0	0
لغاح	*Loo-fáh* Fruit of the mandrake	0	3	0	0
افيون	*Af-yoon* Opium	0	4	0	0
شوكران	*Showkrán* Hemlock	0	4	0	0
لبن خشخاش	*Lebn Khuſhkháſh* Milk of the poppy	0	4	0	0
اصل النيل	*Uſſel ul neel* Root of the *neel* tree	0	0	1	0
بادام شيرين	*Bádám ſhereen* Sweet almond	0	0	1	0
پرسياوشان	*Pir-ſy-ow-ſhán* Maiden hair	0	0	1	0
پوست جوز	*Poaſt jowz* Walnut ſhells	0	0	1	0
تخم خربزه	*Tokhem Khirboozéh* Muſk melon ſeed	0	0	1	0
حب الغار	*Hub ul ghár* Laurel berries	0	0	1	0
اب انجره	*Ab Unjereh* Juice of nettles	0	0	1	0
حزاز الصخر	*Huzáz uſ ſuckher* Moſs that grows on ſtones, &c.	0	0	1	0
دفلي	*Diflee* Rhododaphne	0	0	1	0
رازيانه	*Rázee-áneh* A ſpecies of aniſeed	0	0	1	0
روغن جوز	*Rughen jowz* Oil of walnuts	0	0	1	0
زعفران	*Za-frán* Saffron	0	0	1	0

	NAMES.	QUALITIES. HOT.	COLD.	DRY.	MOIST.
		DEGREES.			
سعد	*Sáád* A prickly plant, of which camels are very fond	0	0	1	0
سويق الشعير	*Seweek us shy-eer* Wheat flour	0	0	0	0
صعتر	*Sá tur* Origanum, or wild marjoram	0	0	1	0
صمغ جوز	*Semugh jowz* Walnut-tree gum	0	0	1	0
ورق سوسن	*Weruck So-sun* Lily leaves	0	0	1	0
اصل المر	*Ussul ul murr* Root of the myrrh tree	0	0	2	0
اصل اللوف	*Ussul ul loof* Root of dragonwort	0	0	2	0
بيخ نيلوفر	*Beykh neeloofir* Root of the water lily	0	0	2	0
حبة الخضرا	*Hubbet-'ul khuzra* Juniper berries	3	0	2	0
زفت	*Zift* Pitch	0	0	2	0
سنبل الطيب	*Sembel ut' teib* Spikenard	0	0	2	0
سنبل رومي	*Sembel roomee* Celtic nard	0	0	2	0
شجره مصطكي	*Shejereh musteká* The mastich tree	0	0	2	0
قفر اليهود	*Kufr-ul yehood* Jew's pitch	0	0	2	0
شيلم	*Sheelum* Tares	2	0	2	0
قشور الاترج	*Ke-shoor-ul-oot-ruj* Citron peel	0	0	2	0
كرنب	*Kirnub* Cabbage	0	0	2	0
كرسنه	*Kur-seneh* Pea	0	0	2	0
لبن	*Lebn* Milk	0	0	2	0
مرمكي	*Murr muck-kee* Mecca myrrh	0	0	3	0
نسج العنكبوة	*Nesj-ul-unkeboot* Cobweb	0	0	2	0
ابهل	*Ub-hel* Seed of the mountain pine	0	0	3	0
اصل فنطافلون	*Ussul fentá-fe-loon* Root of cinquefoil	0	0	3	0

NAMES.		QUALITIES.			
		HOT.	COLD.	DRY.	MOIST.
		DEGREES.			
كرنب خشك	*Kirnub Kooshk* Dried cabbage	0	0	3	0
بوره	*Boorah* Borax	0	0	3	0
پوست غرب سوخته	*Poast gherb Sokkteh* Bark of the mountain pine, burnt	0	0	3	0
حلتيت	*Hil teet* Asafœtida	0	0	3	0
حماض الاترج	*Hum-az ul Ootruj* Citron juice	0	0	3	0
دارشيشعان	*Dár-she-shaén* An aromatic bark of a prickly tree	0	0	3	0
دخن	*Dukhen* A kind of grain resembling millet	0	0	3	0
زباد	*Ze'bad* Civet	0	0	3	0
رماد حلزون بري	*Ré-mád hulzoon bir-ree* Calcined wood-snails	0	0	3	1
روغن ترب	*Roghen toorb* Oil of radish	0	0	3	0
زوفا	*Zoofá* Hyssop	0	0	3	0
سداب بوستاني	*Soodáb bostánee* Garden rue	0	0	3	2
سرطان محرق	*Sirtán Mohruck* Calcined crabs	0	0	3	0
سركه	*Seer-keh* Vinegar	0	0	3	0
شب محرق	*Shub mohruck* Burnt alum	0	0	3	0
شونيز	*Shoo-neez*, commonly called *See-ab daneh*, or black seed	0	0	3	0
صوف محرق	*Soof mohruck* Burnt wool	0	0	3	0
فاوانيا	*Fá-dá-nyá* A root resembling the carrot	0	0	3	0

فاشرا

NAMES.		QUALITIES.			
		HOT.	COLD.	DRY.	MOIST.
		DEGREES.			
فاشرا	*Fá-ſhe-rá* Briony	0	0	3	0
فطراساليون	*Fit-ra ſá-li-yoon* Parſley	0	0	3	0
قيصوم	*Ky-ſoom* Southernweed	0	0	3	0
كرفس بري	*Kerfs bir-ree* Wild parſley	0	0	3	0
مشكطرا مشيع	*Miſk-kee-tara-meſhugh* Dittany of Crete	0	0	3	0
ورق غار	*Werek ghár* Laurel leaves	0	0	3	0
خردل	*Khirdul* Muſtard ſeed	0	0	4	0
كرم	*Kerm* Vine branches	0	0	4	0
برگ بنفشه	*Berg-bé-núf-ſheh* Violet leaves	0	0	0	1
خصية الثعلب	*Khuſeyet us ſáleb* Satyrion	0	0	0	1
عصاره سوسن	*U-ſa-reh ſo-ſun* Expreſſed juice of lillies	0	0	0	1
كاهو	*Ká-hoo* Lettuce	0	0	0	1
لسان الثور	*Liſſán us ſáur* Ox tongue, bugloſs	0	0	0	1
قرع	*Kurá* Gourd with thin rind	0	0	0	2
مشمش	*Miſhmiſh* Apricot	0	0	0	2
دم الاخوين	*Dum ul akhwein* Dragon's blood	0	0	0	1
شجر جوز	*Shejir jowz* Walnut tree	0	0	0	1
فطر	*Fithr* Muſhroom	0	0	0	1
ورق عليق	*Werek Uleik* Bramble leaves	0	2	0	1
اصل الخنثي	*Uſſul ul khunſá* The hermaphrodite root	1	1	0	0
حب الصنوبر	*Hnb us ſonobur* Pine kernels	1	1	0	0
خربزه	*Khirboozeh* Muſk melon	1	1	0	0
زيت	*Ziet* Olive oil	1	1	0	0
زيتون	*Zietoon* Olives	1	1	0	0

سرخس

NAMES.		QUALITIES. HOT.	COLD.	DRY.	MOIST.
		DEGREES.			
سرخس	*Sir-ukhs* Root of ſpleenwort, mule's fern	1	2	0	0
شمع	*Shum-a* Bees' wax	1	1	0	0
طين ساموس	*Teen ſamoos* Samian earth	1	1	0	0
مردارسنك	*Murdárſung* Litharge of lead	1	1	0	0

مخدرات *MOKEDERRÁT.*—NARCOTICA.

اذاراقي *Uzá-rá-kee* Seed of a poiſonous Indian root

اسپند *Is-pund* Wild rue

اصل الذرة *Uſſel uz zooret* Root of a ſpecies of grain, commonly called *jáwirs*

اصل اللفاح *Uſſel ul Loofah* Mandrake root

افيون *Uf yoon* Opium

بيخ موته جنكلي *Beykh mowteh junglee* Root of a ſpecies of graſs

تخم وبرك تنباكو *Tokhem wu berg tumbákoo* Seed and leaves of tobacco

جوزماثل *Jowz mā.ſil* The thorn apple

سراج القطرب *Sé-ráj-ul kootreb* The fairy's lamp: a plant which ſhines at night like the glow-worm

شبيبي *She-bee-bee* A narotic root

شوكران *Shukrān* Hemlock

قنب *Kinnub* Hemp

كاكنج *Kákenj* Winter cherry

لبن الخيل *Lebn ul ki el* Mare's milk

لونك جنكلي *Lowng junglee* Wild cloves

مسهلات صفرا *MOOS-HIL-ÁT SUF-RÁ.*—CHOLAGOGA.

اجاص *Ij jáſs* A ſpecies of plum

افستين *Afsunteen* Wormwood

بنفشه خشك *Beneſſheh Khooſkh* Dried violets

ترنجبين *Tu-renjebeen* A ſpecies of manna

تمرهندي *Temr-hindee* Tamarind

خيارشنبر *Khy-ar-ſhumber* Caſſia fiſtularis

سقمونيا *Suc-mo-nya* Scammony

شاهترة *Shah-tereh* Fumitory

شبرم	*Shibrum* A ſpecies of ſpurge
شيرخشت	*Sheer-khiſht* Manna
صبر	*Sub-ir* Aloes
كلسرخ	*Gool ſoorkh* Red roſes
لبلاب	*Lublâb* Ivy
مازريون	*Mâz-ri-yoon* Mezereon
هليله زرد	*He-ley-leh zird* Yellow myrobolans.

مسهلات بلغم *MOOS-HIL-ÁT BELGHEM.*——PHLEGMAGOGA.

بسفايج	*Bis-fâ-ij* Polypody
تربد	*Toorbood* Turbith root
حب النيل	*Hub ul neel* Berries of a blue creeper
حرمل	*Hirmul* Wild rue
شحم حنظل	*Shêm hênzil* Pulp of colo-quintida
غاريقون	*Ghâ-ree-koon* Agaric
فرفيون	*Fir-fee-yoon* Euphorbium
قثاء الحمار	*Kiſſâ ul hymar* Wild cucumber
قنطوريون	*Kun-too-reeyoon* Centaury
ماهيزهرج	*Mâhee-zeh-ruj* A ſpecies of creeper
ماهودانه	*Mâhoo-dâneh* A ſmall red ſeed called alſo *hub ul mulook*

مسهلات سودا *MOOS-HIL-ÁT SOWDÁ.*——MELANAGOGA.

افتيمون	*Afteemoon* Dodder of thyme
اسطوخودوس	*Us-too-khoo-doos* Stoechas, French lavender
امله	*Á-mu-leh* Emblic myrobolans
بالنكو	*Bâ-lun-goo* A ſpecies of ſweet baſil
بسفايج	*Bisfâ-ij* Polypody
حجر لاجورد	*Hejr lâ'j-wird* Lapis lazuli
سنا	*Sê-nâ* Senna
غاريقون	*Ghâ-ree-koon* Agaric
كشوث	*Koo-ſhoos* The herb curſuta
هليله كابلي	*He-ley-leh câbulee* Chebuli myrobolans

مقيات *MOKI-YE-ÁT.*——EMETICA.

اب كدوي تلخ	*Ãb kud-oo telkh* Juice of bitter gourd
بوره	*Boorah* Borax
تخم وبرك ترب	*Tokhem wu birg toorb* Seed and leaves of radiſh
تخم شبت	*Tokhem Sheb-it* Fennel ſeed

تخم جرجير

E

تخم جرجير	*Tokhem-jir-jeer* Seed of wild rocket	كندش	*Koondoosh* Glaſſwort
تخم مازريون	*Tokhem máz-ri-yoon* Seed of wild ſpurge	لوبياي سرخ	*Loo-beeyá Soorkh* A red pot-herb
خربق	*Khir-buc* Hellebore	ماءالعسل	*Má ul áſſel* Water and honey
سكنجبين	*Si-ken-je-been* Oxymel of vinegar and honey	مويزج	*Mě-wee-zuj* Raiſins
كنكرزد	*Kunkir zud* Artichoke gum	نمك هندي	*Ne-muck hindee* Salt of bitumen.

مفتحات MU-FETTÉ-HÁT.——DEOBSTRUENTIA.

اذخر	*Iz-keir* Camel's hay	شاهترا	*Shah-tereh* Fumitory
اسطوخودوس	*Us-too-koo-doos* Stoechas	صعتر	*Sââ-tur* Origany, or wild thyme
افتيمون	*Afteemoon* Dodder of thyme	عود	*Oowd* Lignum aloes
افسنتين	*Áfsunteen* Wormwood	غاريقون	*Ghâ-ree-koon* Agaric
انيسون	*Á-nee-ſoon* Aniſeed	فراسيون	*Frâ-ſee-yoon* Euphraſia, eye-bright
ايرسا	*Iyr-ſa* Root of blue Iris	قردمانا	*Koor-du-mâ-nâ* Cardmine
ترمس	*Toormiſs* Egyptian lupin	قنطوريون	*Kun-too-ree-yoon* Centaury
جنطيانا	*Gen-ti-â-ná* Gentian	كبابه	*Ku-bá-beh* Cubebs
حاشا	*Há-ſhá* Thyme	كرفس	*Kereſs* Parſley
حرمل	*Hirmul* Wild rue	كرسنه	*Kir-us-neh* Peas
حماما	*Hě-má-mâ* Amomum	كشوث	*Koo-ſhooſs* The herb curſuta
دارچيني	*Dár-chee-nee* Cinnamon	مرزنجوش	*Mir-zun-jooſh* Marjoram
رازيانه	*Ra-ze:-á neh* A ſpecies of aniſeed	نانخواه	*Nân-khûh* A ſpecies of cumin ſeed
زراوند	*Zir-a-wund* Birthwort	هليون	*Hul-yoon* Aſparagus
زعفران	*Zâ-frân* Saffron		
زيرا	*Zee-ra* Cumin ſeed		

ملطفات

ملطفات *MU-LUTTIFAT.*—ATTENUANTIA.

ابهل	*Ub-kel* Fruit of the plane tree	خردل	*Khir-dul* Mustard feed
اذخر	*Iz-keir* Camel's hay	دارچيني	*Dâr-chee-nee* Cinnamon
اسطوخودوس	*Us-too-khoo-doos* Stoechas	زراوند	*Zir-â-wund* Birthwort
اشقيل	*Iss-keel* Squills	زوفاخشک	*Zoofâ-khooshk* Hyssop
اقحوان	*Ok hy-wân* Lovage	سداب	*Sudâb* Rue
انجره	*Un-je reh* Nettle	سرکه	*Seer-keh* Vinegar
ايرسا	*Iyr-sa* Root of blue Iris	سکبينج	*Sug-bee-nuj* Sagapenum
بابونه	*Bá-boo-neh* Camomile flowers	سير	*Seer* Garlic
بوره	*Boo-reh* Borax	صعتر	*Sââ-tur* Origany
پودنه	*Pow-de-neh* Mint	عاقرقرحا	*Akir-kir-hâ* Pellitory
جعده	*Joâ-deh* A species of wormseed	فنجنکشت	*Funj-ungoosht* The chaste tree
جندبيدستر	*Joond-bey-duster* Civet	قردمانا	*Koor-du-mâ-nâ* Cardmine
حاشا	*Hâ-shâ* Thyme	قرطم	*Koor-tim* Safflower, bastard saffron
حب البان	*Hub-ul-bân* Ben nuts	مشکطرامشيع	*Mishkê-toorû-mish-eeyâ* Dittany.
حرف	*Hoorf* Seed of Garden cresses	کمادريوس	*Ku-mâ-dree-yoos* Germander.
حرمل	*Hirmul* Wild rue		
حماض	*Hum-âz* Sorrel		

مدرات *MU-DORRÂT*—STIMULANTIA.

ابهل	*Ukkel* Fruit of the plane tree	برنجاسف	*Bir-un-jâ-sif* Mugwort
اقحوان	*Ok-hywân* Lovage	بابونه	*Bâ-boo-neh* Camomile flowers
انجدان	*Un je-dân* The seed of the asafoetida plant	پرسياوشان	*Pir-sy ow-shân* Maiden hair
انيسون	*Â-nee soon* Aniseed	تخم کزر	*Tokhem Guz-ir* Carrot seed

ترس·

ترمس *Toor-miſs* Egyptian lupin

جاوشير *Já-wē-ſheer* Gum opopanax

جعده *Joâ-deh* A ſpecies of wormſeed

جندبيدستر *Joond-bey-duſter* Civet

حبة الخضرا *Hubbet-ül khŭz–rab* Fruit of the turpentine tree

نانخواه *Nán-khâb* A ſpecies of cumin ſeed

دارچيني *Dár-chee-nee* Cinnamon

رازيانه *Rá-zee-âneh* A ſpecies of aniſeed

زوفاءِ خشك *Zoofa Khooſkh* Hyſſop

سداب *Sudáb* Rue

سعد *Saad* A prickly graſs

سليخه *Sĕ-lee-kheb* Caſſia lignum

شونيز *Show-neez* A ſmall black ſeed

عروق *Ou-rook* Sulphur

بابونه *Bá-booneh* Camomile flowers

عود *Owd* Lignum aloes

فراسيون *Frâ-see-yoon* Euphraſia, eye-bright

قردمانا *Koor-du-má-ná* Cardmine

قسط *Coſt* Coſtus

قنطوريون *Kun-tooryoon* Centaury

كبابه *Kub-á-beh* Cubebs

كرفس *Kerefs* Parſley

كمادريوس *Kum-á-dry-oos* Germander

مرزنجوش *Mir-zun-jooſh* Marjoram

مشكطرامشيع *Miſhké-toorá–my-ſheé-á* Dittany

ميعه *Mee-áb* Storax

نمام *Ne-mám* Mother of thyme.

مفتتات *MU-FUTTE-TAT*.—LITHONTRIPTICA.

اسارون *Á-ſa-roon* Aſarabacca

بادام تلخ *Bá-dám telkh* Bitter almond

برنجاسب *Bir-un-ja-ſif* Mugwort

پرسياوشان *Pir-ſy-ow-ſhān* Maiden hair

تخم خربزه خشك *Tokhem Khurboozeh khooſhk* Dried muſk-melon ſeed

حجر اليهود *Hejr-ul-yehood* Jew's ſtone

رازيانه *Rá-zee-á-neh* A ſpecies of aniſeed

سعد *Saád* A prickly graſs

سكبينج *Sug-bee-nuj* Sagapenum

صمغ آلو *Sum-egh áloo* Plum-tree gum

نخود سياه *Nákhood ſy-ah* A ſpecies of vetch

قابضات

قابضات *KĀ-BIZ-ĀT.*—ASTRINGENTIA.

اذخر	*Iz-kheir* Camel's hay
امرود	*Umrood* Pear
باقلا	*Bá-ke-lá* Beans
بيخ بارتنك	*Beykh Bâr-tung* Root of ribwort
برنج	*Bê-runj* Rice.
ورق زر	*Werek zir* Gold leaf
بلوط	*Beloot* Acorns
بسد	*Boo-ſud* Coral
تخم شاهسفرم	*Tokhem ſhâhus-fe-rum* Seed of ſweet baſil
تخم كل	*Tokhem gool* Roſe ſeed
جوز سرو	*Jowz ſir-oe* Fruit of the cypreſs tree
دم الاخوين	*Dum ul akhwein* Dragon's blood
زعرور	*Za-roor* Medlars
سماق	*Su-māk* Sumach
طباشير	*Te-bâ-ſheer* Sugar of bamboe
طين مختوم	*Teen Mukhtoom* Sealed earth
عدس	*Ud-us* A ſpecies of vetch
كرويا	*Kur-wee-ya* Caraway ſeed
كندر	*Koondir* Frankincenſe
كهربا	*Keh-robā* Amber
كاورس	*Gâ-wirs* A ſpecies of vetch
مصطكي	*Moos-tē-kā* Gum maſtich
مورد	*Mow-rud* Myrtle
ناردين	*Nārdeen* Celtic nard
نشاسته	*Nē-ſhâs-teh* Starch
نبق	*Nibk* A ſpecies of lote
نخود	*Nekhood* A ſpecies of vetch

محللات *MO-HELIL-ĀT.*—DISCUTIENTIA.

اذخر	*Iz-kheir* Camel's hay
اسقيل	*Is-keel* Squills
اسارون	*A-sâ-roon* Aſarabacca
اشق	*Ouſhuc* Gum ammoniacum
اقحوان	*Ok-hywān* Lovage
اكليل الملك	*Ukleel ul mē-lic* Melilot
باقلا	*Bá-ke-lá* A ſpecies of bean
بابونه	*Bá-boo-neh* Camomile flowers
برنجاسف	*Bir-un-ja-ſif* Mugwort
پرسياوشان	*Pir-ſy-ow-ſhân* Maiden hair
پودنه	*Powdeneh* Mint
ترمس	*Toor-miſs* Egyptian lupin
جعده	*Joe-deh* A ſpecies of wormſeed
جاوشير	*Já-we-ſheer* Gum opopanax

حاشا *Há-ſhá* Thyme

خرزهره *Khir-zereb* Rhododaphne

خروع *Khir wá* Palma chriſti

خطمي *Khit-mee* A ſpecies of Mallows

روباه تربك *Robah-tirbuc* A ſpecies of nightſhade

زراوند *Zir-á-wund* Birthwort

زفت *Zift* Pitch

سوسن *So-ſun* Lily

صمغ بطم *Sumegh bootem* Gum of the turpentine tree

غار *Ghár* Laurel

قثا *Kiſſa* The long cucumber

قنه *Koon-neh* Galbanum

كبر *Kub-ir* Capers

كمات *Ké-mát* A ſpecies of fungus

لادن *Lá-dun* The herb labdanum

كمادريوس *Kemá-dryoos* Germander

مرزنجوش *Mir-zun-jooſh* Marjoram

نمام *Nimám* Mother of thyme

منضجات *MUN-ZIJ-ÁT*—SUPPURANTIA.

اكليل الملك *Ukleel ul melic* Melilot

انجير *Unjeer* Figs

ايرسا *Iyr-ſa* Root of blue Iris

برك خطمي *Birg Khitmee* Mallow leaves

زعفران *Zá-frán* Saffron

صمغ بطم *Sumegh bootem* Gum of the turpentine tree

كرنب *Kir-nub* Cabbage

لادن *Lá-dun* Labdanum

مر *Murr* Myrrh

مرورشك *Mirwir-ſhuck* An odoriferous graſs

موم *Moom* Bees' wax

ميعه *Mee-áh* Storax

مفشيات *MO-FE-SHY-AT*—CARMINATIVA.

افتيمون *Afteemoon* Dodder of thyme

انيسون *A-nee-ſoon* Aniſeed

بسباسه *Biſs-lá-ſeb* Mace

پنجنكشت *Punj-ungooſht* Agnus caſtus

تخم كزر *Tokhem guz-zir* Carrot ſeed

جاوشير *Já-we-ſheer* Opopanax

حماما *Hê-má-má* Amomum

دارفلفل *Dár fifil* Long pepper

زراوند *Zir-á-wund* Birthwort

زرنباد *Zir-em-bád* Zedoary

زنجبيل *Zunjebeel* Dried ginger

زيره *Zee-rah* Cumin feed

سداب *Sudáb* Rue

سعد *Saad* Roots of a fpecies of grafs

صعتر *Sá-tur* Origany

فلفل *Filfil* Black pepper

قردمانا *Koor-du-má-ná* Cardmine

كرفس *Kerefs* Parfley

نانخواه *Nán-kháh* A fpecies of Wormfeed

مقويات دماغ *MO-KE-WY-ÁT DEMÁGH*——CEPHALICA.

آملج *Ám-luj* Emblic Myrobolans

انفحه ضان *Unfekheh zán* Rennet of an ewe

بالنكو *Bá-lun-goo* A fpecies of fweet bafil

بلادر *Bé-lá-door* Anacardium, Malacca bean

بندق *Bin-dook* Filberts

بهاربه وامرود وسيب *Báhár beeh wu umrood wu feeb* Bloffoms of quinces, pears, and apples

دماغ حيوانات *Demágh hywán-át* The brains of animals

روغن عنبر *Roghen umbir* Oil of ambergris

زنجبيل *Zun-je-beel* Dried ginger

سعد *Saad* Roots of a fpecies of grafs

سيب *Seeb* Apples

سنبل *Sembul* Spikenard

شربت نارنج *Shirbut nárenj* Orange fherbet

عود *Owd* Lignum aloes

عنبر *Umbir* Ambergris

غاليه *Gha-leah* A compofition of mufk, ambergris, camphor, and oil of ben nuts

قرنفل *Kir-un-ful* Cloves

كندر *Koondir* Frankincenfe

كل سرخ *Gool Soorkh* Red rofes

لبن ضان *Lebn zán* Ewe's milk

لحم دراج *Lehm dir-ráj* The flefh of quail

لحم دجاج *Lehm Dujaj* Flefh of the houfe hen

ماءالورد *Má-ul-wird* Rofe Water

مشك *Moofhk* Mufk

نسرين *Nuffreen* The wild rofe

ياسمين *Ye-ás-meen* Jafmine

ابريشم

مقويات دل *MO-KÉ-WY-ÁT DIL.*—CARDIACA.

- ابريشم *Ub-rey-ſhem* Raw ſilk
- اترج *Ut-rej* Citron
- اسطوخودوس *Is-too-khoodoos* Stoechas
- امرود *Umrood* Pears
- امله *Ám-leh* Emblic myrobalans
- انار شيرين *Ánár ſhereen* Sweet pomegranates
- بادروج *Bádrooj* A ſpecies of ſweet baſil
- بالنکو *Bá-lun-goo* An odoriferous plant
- بسفايج *Bis-fa-yej* Polypody
- بسد *Boos-ſud* Coral
- به *Beeh* Quince
- پوست اترج *Poaſt Utrij* Citron peel
- تمرهندي *Temr-hindee* Tamarind
- جدوار *Jedwár* A ſpecies of ginger
- دارچيني *Dár-chee-nee* Cinnamon
- درونج *Diroo-nuj* A root reſembling the tail of a ſcorpion
- ريباس *Ree-báſs* Rhapontic
- زرنباد *Zir-um-bad* Zedoary
- زعفران *Zá-frán* Saffron
- سعد *Saad* Roots of a ſpecies of graſs
- سليخه *Si-lee-kheh* Caſſia lignea
- سنبل *Sembul* Spikenard
- سوسن *So-ſun* Lily
- سيب *Seeb* Apples
- شقاقل *She-ká-kul* Wild carrot
- صندل *Sundel* Sandal wood
- طباشير *Te-bá-ſheer* Sugar of bamboo
- طين مختوم *Teen Mukhtoom* Sealed earth
- عنبر *Umbir* Ambergris
- عود *Ood* Lignum aloes
- فرنجمشک *Ferenjmooſhk* An odoriferous plant
- قاقله *Ká-ke-leh* Cardamums
- کافور *Ká-foor* Camphor
- کشنيز خشک *Kiſhneez khooſhk* Dried coriander ſeed
- کهربا *Keh-ro-bá* Amber
- گاوزبان *Gow-ze-bán* Bugloſs, ox tongue
- گلسرخ *Gool ſoorkh* Red roſe
- لاجورد *Láj-wird* Lapis lazuli
- لولو *Loo-loo* Pearl
- مورد *Mow-rud* Myrtle
- نمام *Ne-mám* Mother of thyme
- نارمشک *Nár-mooſhk* A fragrant flower, commonly called *ná-giſſir*
- نعناع *Ná-naá* Spearmint

نيلوفر

نيلوفر *Nee-loo-fir* Water lily

ورق زر و نقره *Werek zir wu nokerah* Gold and silver leaf

هليله *He-lee-leh* Yellow myrobalans

ياقوت *Yá-coot* Ruby

معويات كبد *MO-KÉ-WY-AT KÉBID.*—HEPATICA.

اشنه *Oushneh* Dodder of oak, &c.

اظفا الطيب *Uzfár ul teib* Perfumed nails

جوزبوا *Jowz bu-wá* Nutmeg

حب البلسان *Hubul Bulesán* Carpobalsam

حماما *Humámá* Amomum

دارچيني *Dárcheenee* Cinnamon

غافث *Ghá-fis* Hemp agrimony

قرنفل *Ke-run-full* Cloves

قرفه *Kirfeh* An odoriferous thick bark, of the colour of cloves, which it also resembles in smell, and is therefore also called *Ki-fetül ke-run-full*, or *bark of cloves:* another species is thinner, of a brighter red, and sweeter to the taste, resembling small pieces of cinnamon, but the first kind is preferable.

كشوث *Ku-shoos* A species of Dodder

مصطكي *Mustī-ká* Mastich

ناردين *Nárdain* Celtic nard

معويات معده *MO-KÉ-WY-ÁT ME-OA-DEH.*—TONICA.

امله *Ám-leh* Emblic myrobalans

اذخر *Iz-kier* Camel's hay

بالنكو *Bálungoo* A species of sweet basil

بليله *Be-le-leh* Belleric myrobalans

پوست ترنج *Poast Turenj* Citron peel

جوزبوا *Jowz-bu-wá* Nutmeg

دارچيني *Dárcheenee* Cinnamon

زرنباد *Zer-em-bád* Zedoary

سادج هندي *Sádij hindee* Indian leaf

سعد *Sáád* Roots of a species of grass

سفرجل *Suf-er-jel* Quince

سليخه *Se-lee-kheh* Cassia lignea

سماق *Sumák* Sumach

طباشير *Te-bá-sheer* Sugar of bamboe

قاقله *Ká-ku-leh* Cardamoms

قرنفل *Ke-run full* Cloves

قرفه *Kirf.h* An odoriferous bark, *vide supra*

كل سرخ *Geol soorkh* Red rose

كرويا

كرويا *Kur-wee-yá* Caraways

كندر *Koondir* Frankincenſe

مشكطرامشيع *Miſk-ketrá-meſhyá* Dittany

مصطكي *Mus-té-ká* Maſtich

نعناع *Na-náá* Mother of thyme

هليله *He-lee-leh* Yellow myrobalans

مبهيات *MO-BÉHY-ÁT.*——APHRODISIACA.

انجير *Injeer* Figs

رطب *Ru-teb* Freſh dates

بسباسه *Bir-báſsá* Mace

انكور *Ungoor* Grapes

باقلا *Bá-kē-lá* A ſpecies of bean

بيضه كبوتر *Byzēh ke-boo-tir* Pigeon's eggs

بيضه كبك *Byzēh Kubk* Partridge's eggs

بيضه كنجشك *Byzēh kunjeſhk* Sparrow's eggs

پنير مايه شتر *Pun-eer-máyeh ſhootir* Rennet of a camel

جرجير *Jir-jeer* A kind of bean

چلغوزه *Chulghoozeh* Fruit of the mountain pine

حبة الخضرا *Hubletūl khuzrū* Fruit of the turpentine tree

حلتيت *Hilteet* Aſafœtida

خصية الثعلب *Khuſſyet 'l' ſáleb* Satyrion

خولنجان *Khoolinján* Galangal

دارچيني *Dárcheenee* Cinnamon

زرنباد *Zur-em búd* Zedoary

زنجبيل *Zunjibeel* Dried ginger

سقنقور *Sue'-un-koor* Skink

سورنجان *Soor-in-ján* Hermodactyls

شقاقل *Shē-ká-kul* Wild carrot

شير ميش *Sheer meeſh* Ewe's milk

فستق *Fis-took* Piſtachio nuts

فندق *Findook* Filberts

قرنه *Kir feh* An odoriferous bark, vide *Hepatica*

قسط *Kuſt* Coſtus

كثيرا *Ke ſee-rá* Gum tragacanth

اكر *Ig-gir* Sweet-ſcented flag

كرفس *Kerefs* Parſley

كنجد *Kun-jid* Seſamé

كزر *Guz ir* Carrot

لوبيا *Loo-by á* A ſpecies of bean

مغز جوز *Meghz jowz* Peeled walnuts

مغز بادام *Meghz Bā-dām* Bleeched almonds

مغز دماغ كنجشك وبره *Meghz demagh khunjiſhk wu bu reh* Brains of ſparrows, and of kid

نارجيل *Nár-jeel* Cocoa nut

هليون *Halyoon* Aſparagus

نخود *Nukhood* A ſpecies of vetch

مسكنات اوجاع

مسكنات اوجاع MO-SUCKEN-ÁT OWJÁ.—ANODYNA.

اسفيداج *Is-fy.dáj* White lead

افيون *Ufi-oon* Opium

بيخ بيروج *Beykh Beyrooj* Root of the mandrake

پيه بط *Peeb but* Goose grease

تورك *Tooruck* Purslain

سفيده تخم مرغ *Sefeydeb tokhem murgh* White of egg

صمغ عربي *Semegh árebee* Gum Arabic

كثيرا *Ke-see-ra* Gum tragacanth

نشاسته *Neshásteh* Starch

مسبتات MO-SÉ-BÉ-TÁT.—HYPNOTICA.

اصطرك *Us-te-ruck* Storax

اقحوان *Owk-ky-wán* Lovage

حماما *Hamá-má* Amomum

زعفران *Záf-rān* Saffron

شاهسفرم *Shábusferem* Sweet basil

شبت *Shib-it* Fennel

شقايق *She-ká-yik* Anemone

حلتيت *Hilteet* Asafœtida

كاهو *Kà-hu* Lettuce

لفاح *Lu-fah* Fruit of the mandrake

مرو *Merwo* A berry

قاطعات ديدان. KÁ-TÉ-ÁAT DEE-DAN.—ANTHELMINTICA.

اثمد *Is-mud* Native antimony

افسنتين *Afsunteen* Wormwood

برنج كابلي *Beerunj Cábulee* A black seed resembling pepper, only smaller; it is white within-side, and a little bitter

جعده *Joa-deb* A species of wormseed

زوفاي خشك *Zoofa khooshk* Hyssop.

مانعات رعاف واسهال الدم MÁ-NYÁT RO-ÁF WU ISS-HÁL-UD'-DUM. STYPTICA.

اثمد *Is-mud* Native antimony

بادروج *Bád-rooj* A species of sweet basil

بزر البنج *Buz-ir 'ul Bunj* Henbane seed

بلوط *Zebot* Acorns

تخم كل	*Tokhem gool* Rose seed	كشنيز	*Kishneez* Coriander seed
جوزسرو	*Jowz sir-oe* Fruit of the cypress tree	كهربا	*Keh-ro-bá* Amber
حضض	*Hu-zuz* Juice of buck thorn	كلنار	*Goolnár* Flowers of the fruitless pomegranate
دم الخوين	*Dum-ul-ábkwain* Dragon's blood	كل ارمني	*Gil urmenee* Bole armenic
ريوند	*Rey-wend* Rhapontic, wild rhubarb	لسان الحمل	*Lissán ul heml* Ribwort, or plantain
زرشك	*Zir-ushk* Barberries	مازو	*Má-zou* Gall apple
زيره	*Zeerah* Cumin seed	مصطكي	*Musté-ká* Mastich
شادنه	*Shá-dē-neh* Bloodstone	نشاسته	*Neshásteh* Starch
قنطوريون	*Kun-teeryoon* Centaury	نعناع	*Na-náá* Mother of thyme
كافور	*Ká-foor* Camphor		

مقرحات *MO-KÉ-RE-HÁT.*——VESCEATORIA

اسقيل	*Is-keil* Squills	سداب	*Sud-áb* Rue
اهك	*Ábuck* Quick lime	سنباده	*Sum-bá-deh* Emery stone
بورق	*Booruc* Borax	صابون	*Sá-boon* Soap
حرف	*Hoorf* Seed of garden cresses	فربيون	*Fir-byoon* Euphorbium
ذراريح	*Ze-rá-reeb* Cantharides	قسط	*Kust* Costus
راسن	*Rá-sun* Elecampane	قلقطارسبز	*Kul-kē-trá subz* Green vitriol
زاج	*Zaj* White vitriol	لبن يتوع	*Lebn ye-tua* Milky juice of plants
زرنيخ	*Zir-neikh* Arsenic		

مدملات قروح *MO-DUM-IL-ÁT KE-ROUH.*——CICATRIZANTIA.

اثمد	*Is-mud* Native antimony	ايرسا	*Iyr-sa* Iris root
اسرنج	*Iss-renj* Red lead	دم الاخوين	*Dumuläkhwain* Dragon's blood

انزروت

انزروت	*Unzeroot* Sorcocolla	طین مختوم	*Teen mukhtoom* Sealed earth
زراوند	*Zir-á-wend* Birthwort	عسل	*Aſſul* Honey
زیره	*Zeerah* Cumin ſeed	گلنار	*Goolnár* Pomegranate bloſſoms
صبر	*Syb-ir* Aloes	لسان الحمل	*Liſſan ul hĕmil* Ribwort
صمغ آلو	*Semegh aloo* Plum-tree gum	ورق بلوط	*Werek beloot* Oak leaves

مجليات اوساخ قروح *MOJELLYÁT OWSÁK KEROUH.*—DETERGENTIA.

ابهل	*Ubhel*	حب بلسان	*Hub buleſán* Carpobalſam
آبكامه	*Ab-ká-meh* A compoſition of milk curds, and ſeed of wild rue, prepared with leaven and vinegar	راتینج	*Rá-te-nej* Reſin
		زفت	*Ziſt* Pitch
		عسل	*Aſſul* Honey
ابرسا	*Iyr-ſa* Iris root	نمک	*Nĕ-muck* Salt

اكال كوشت زياده قروح *ÁKÁL GOWSHT ZYADEH KEROUH.*-CAUSTICA.

انزروت	*Unzeroot* Sorcocolla	صوف سوخته	*Soof ſowkhteh* Burnt wool
توبال مس	*Tobál miſs* Blue vitriol	مردار سنگ	*Murdár ſung* Litharge of lead
زنگار	*Zun-gár* Verdegris		

يابسات قروح *YA-BIS-AT KEROUH.*——EPULOTICA.

اشنه	*Ouſhneh* Moſs of pine, and other trees	آهک شسته	*Ábuck ſhoos-teh* Slacked lime
		توتیا	*Too ty-á* Tutty
خرماي سوخته	*Khoorma ſokhteh* Burnt dates	صبر	*Syb-ir* Aloes
انزروت	*Unzeroot* Sorcocolla	صوف سوخته	*Soof Sokhteh* Burnt wool

پوست انار	*Poaſt ûnâr* Pomegranate peel	سرکه و نوشادر و نمک	*Seer-keh wu nowſhâdir, wu nemuck* A mixture of vinegar, ſal ammoniac, and ſalt
زاگ سوخته	*Zâg ſowkhteh* Burnt alum	سورنجان	*Soor in-jân* Hermodactyls
زنکار با سپیده بیضه مرغ سرشته	*Zun-gâr bâ ſepeydeh Byzeh murgh ſeriſhteh* Verdegris with white of egg	صعتر	*Sâ-tur* Origany

ادويه هيضه *ADVIYAH HEE-ZEH.*——STOMACHICA.

ابي و سيب بريان كرده	*Áb-ee wu ſeeb be-ryân kirdeh* Fried quinces and apples	اقراص الطين	*Ákrâſs'ut teen* Lozenges made of boles
اب ابي ترش	*Âb âb-ee toorſh* Juice of four quinces	سويق	*Se-weyk* Fried barley
اب سيب كوهي	*Âb ſeeb kuhee* Juice of crab apple	حب الرمان	*Hub'ul rum-mân* Pomegranate ſeeds
اقراص مورد	*Ákrâſs moorud* Myrtle lozenges	شراب ميوها	*Sherâb meywâ-bâ* All kinds of fruit wines
اقراص كندر	*Ákrâſs koondir* Frankincenſe lozenges	صندل و گلاب	*Sundul wu goolâb* Sandâl wood and roſe water
اقراص راسن	*Ákrâſs râ ſun* Elecampane lozenges	مورد و گلاب	*Moorud wû goolâb* Myrtle and roſe water

WEIGHTS.

WEIGHTS.

حبه	*Hubbeh, a.* equal to one جو *jow*, or common barley-corn.	
تسو	*Tussoo, a.* — —	2 barley-corns.
قيراط	*Keerát, a.* or *carat*, —	4 barley-corns.
كهونكچي	*Ghungchy, h.*	— 8 barley-corns.
سرخ	*Soorkh, h.* -	
رتي	*Rutty, h.* -	
ماشه	*Máshah, h.* — —	8 rutties.
توله	*Tolah, h.* — —	12 maſhahs.
تانك	*Tánk, h.* — —	4 maſhahs.
دانك	*Dáng, p.* OR	— — $4\frac{1}{6}$ rutties.
دانق	*Dánek, a.*	
درم	*Direm, p.* OR	— 1 maſhah and 1 rutty.
درهم	*Dirhem, a.*	
مثقال	*Miskál, a.* —	4 maſhahs and $3\frac{1}{2}$ rutties.
استار	*Istár, a.* OR	$1\frac{1}{2}$ tolahs and 2 maſhahs.
سيرشاهي	*Seer Shahy, h.* or, *royal seer.*	
اوقيه	*Owkyáh, a* OR	— $7\frac{1}{2}$ miſkals.
وقيه	*Wekyáh, a.*	
من طبي	*Mun tibby, a.*	40 iſtars.

ULFÁZ UDWIYEH.

THE

MATERIA MEDICA.

ABBREVIATIONS.

a. Arabic. *g.* Greek. *ſy.* Syriac. *p.* Perſian. *h.* Hindevy. *v.* ordinary name. *qu.* quality. 1, 2, 3, 4, degrees. *prop.* medical properties. *ch.* what part or kind to be choſen. *cor.* correctors. *d.* doſe. *ſuc.* ſuccedaneum.

---

(1) آرغيس AARGHEES. *g.* Bark of the root of the barberry buſh.

پوست بیخ درخت زرشک

p. poſt beykh diruckt ze-ruſhk.

(2) اطريلال A-TEREE-LÁL. Crow-foot.

تخم خلال خليل . رجل الغراب

a. *rejel ul gherab.* p. *tokhem khelál khelell.* काकजंगी मीसी

h. *kàkjungee,* and alſo *miſſee.*

qu. hot and dry 2. *ch.* the ſeed.

(3) آلسن Á-LE-SUN. Wild rue.

p. *ſepund ſowkhtenee.* سپند سوختني

(4) ابوخلسا ABOO KHULSÁ. A ſpecies of bugloſs.

p. *ſhunkàr.* شنكار

qu. hot and dry 2. *ch.* black, with many leaves, and thick root. *d.* as far as 2 direms.

(5) ابركاكيا ABERKÁKYÁ. *a.* Cobweb.

मकरे का जाला تنيده عنكبوت

p. *teneedeh unkáboot.* h. *muckree ká jála.*

prop. uſed to ſtop bleeding at the noſe; and applied to green wounds that are ſuperficial.

(6) ابن الماء IBN-UL-MÁ. *a.* Any water fowl.

p. *mor-*

p. *murghábee.* مرغابي

The flesh is heating.

(7) آبست A-BIST. *a.* Pulp of citron.

كوشت ترنج बजोरेकागोद

p. *gowsht turenj.* h. *bee-jowrè-ká good.*

qu. hot and moist 1. *ch.* the species called *bálung.* vide 140.

(8) آبار A-BAR. *a.* Burnt lead.

बंग سرب سوخته

h. *bung.* p. *soorbsowkhteh.*

qu. cold and dry 2. *suc.* native antimony.

(9) ابقر UB-KIR. *a.* Nitre.

बाजी h. *bá-jee.* p. *shooreh.* شوره

(10) ابرار UB-RÁR. *a.* Houseleek.

p. *hy-ul-aalum.* حي العالم

(11) ابن طاهر IBN TAHIR. *a.* Partridge.

p. *kubk.* كبك

(12) آبنوس ÁBNOOS. *a.* Ebony.

p. *áw-noos.* آونوس

qu. hot and dry 2. *prop.* astringent and pungent. *ch.* black, and that will sink in water. *cor.* gum Arabic with sweet basil. *suc.* konar wood; or burnt date seed.

(13) ابو علس ABOO ULS. *a.* Name of a flower.

p. *gool khyree.* گل خيري

qu. hot and dry 1. *prop.* drawing. *ch.* fresh gathered. *d.* a very small quantity. *cor.* yolk of egg.

(14) ابن عرس IBN URS. *a.* The mungoose.

निवोल h. *neywul.* p. *rásoo.* راسو

qu. flesh hot and dry. *prop.* attenuant. *ch.* that which is well covered with hair. *d.* one direm to one miskál, mixed with salt, may be taken to prevent the effects of pestilential air. *cor.* oils. *suc.* rennet, in cases of the epilepsy.

(15) آبق ÁBUC. *a.* Mercury.

पारा h. *pá-ra.* p *seem-áb.* سيماب

(16) ابهرك UBH-RUCK. Talc.

p. *tulc.* طلق

(17) ابهل UBHEL. *a.* The seed of the plane tree, and of the mountain pine.

होबीर تخم وهل - تخم سرو كوهي

p. *tokhem wowhel* and *tokhem sir-œ-kouhee.* h. *howh-beer.*

qu. hot and dry. 3 *prop.* diaphoretic and attenuant, and good for cleaning ulcers. *ch.* black and large, gathered from a tree with leaves of a golden colour. *d.* from two direms to a miskál. *cor.* lignum aloes, or galangal, or amomum, or barberries. *suc.* cypress kernels; or an equal weight of cassia lignea; or one and half direms of cinnamon.

(18) ابل EBIL. The lesser cardamom.

p. *ká-ke-leb seghár.* قاقله صغار

(19) ابابيل Á-BA-BEEL. *a* The swallow.

सपाबीनी پرستوك

h. *se-pa-*

h. *se-pà-bee-nee.* p. *pur-us-took.*

(20) ابريسم EB-REY-SUM. Raw silk.

पाट h. *paut,h.* p. *ebreyshum.* ابريشم

(21) ابرون ABROON. House leek.

p. *hy-ul-áálum.* حي العالم

(22) آبكون ABGOON. Starch.

गेहोंकाहीर نشاسته

h. *geehoon-ká-heer.* p. *neshásteh.*

(23) ابرارالقطه ABRÁR ULKUT-EH. Seed of house leek.

p. *tokhem hy ul áálum.* تخم حي العالم

(24) ابرهيميه IB-RE-HY-MEYAH. A kind of broth.

(25) آبكامه AB-KÁ-MEH. Bread soaked in water, and kept in the sun till it becomes sour.

h. *kàn-jee.* कांजी

(26) آبكينه AB-GEE-NEH. Glass.

कांच h. *kàntch.* p. *sheesheh.* شيشه

(27) ابن حبه IBN HUBBEH. *a.* Bread.

रोटी h. *roo-tee.* p. *nán.* نان

(28) ابي A-BEE. Quince

बिही سفرجل

p. h. *be-hee.* a. *suf-ir-jel.*

(29) ابن آوي IBN A-WEE. The jackal.

सीयाल — गीदर شغال

h. *see-ál* and *gee-dir.* p. *sheghál.*

(30) اترج UT-REJ. Citron.

बिजोरा h. *beyjowrá.* p. *turenj.* ترنج

qu. the peel is hot and dry 2; the inner white coat, hot and moist 1; the juice, cold and dry 2; the seed, hot and moist. *prop.* cardaic, tonic, attenuant, and diaphoretic. *ch.* large, with yellow skin. *d.* for the bite of a scorpion, two miskáls of the seed may be taken infused in hot water.

(31) اترار UT-RÁR. Barberries.

p. *zer-ushk.* زرشك

qu. cold and dry. *ch.* those that are transparent.

(32) اتناميس ÁT-NÁ-MEES. Wild camomile.

p. *bábooneh burree.* بابونه بري

(33) اتان UT-ÀN. A she ass.

गदहि ماده خر

h. *gud-e-hee.* p. *má-deh khur.*

(34) اثمد IS-MUD. *a.* Native antimony.

अंजन سنك سرمه

h. *unjen.* p. *sung sirmeh.*

qu. cold 1, dry 2. *prop.* drying and styptic. *ch.* bright and brittle. *cor.* sugar, and coriander seed. *sue.* burnt lead.

(35) اثلق US-LUC. *a.* Seed of agnus castus.

संभालोके बिज

सम्भालो के बीज تخم پنجنکشت
h. *sem-bhá-loo ké beej.* p. *tokhem punj-ungoosht.*

(36) اثل US-EL. The tamarisk bush.
झाओ h. *j-há-ou.* p. *guz.* گز

(37) اجل كيا AJEL GEE-A. *a.* A poisonous root.
बिस h. *bis.* p *beesh.* بيش

(38) اجمود UJ-MOOD. अजमोद A species of parsley.
p. *buz-ir-ul keress.* بزرالكرفس

(39) اجاص E-JÁSS. A species of plum.
आरो h. *ároo.* p. *a-loo.* آلو

prop. emollient, and a good purgative of the bile.

(40) آجر A-JUR. Burnt bricks.
लकौरीईंट خشت پخته
h. *luck-howree-eent.* p. *khisht pokhteh.*

prop. drying. *ch.* those that are new. *d.* one miskál of the oil of bricks. *cor.* oil of violets. *s.* tiles.

(41) اجواين UJ-WÁ-IN. अजवायन A species of aniseed.
p' *nan-khak.* نانخواه

In Hindevy it moreover is called *jé-wá-én.*

(42) اجواين خراساني *h.* UJ-WA-IN KHORASANY. अजवायनखुरासानी Henbaneseed.
بزرالبنج p. *buz-ir-ul bunj.*

(43) احلب دياي رومي EH-LUBDYA ROOMEE. A species of spurge.
v. *shib-rim.* شبرم

(44) احريض EH-REEZ. Safflower.
कोसम्भ: كاجيره
h. *kosumbh* v. *kájee-reh.*

(45) احداق المرضي EH-DAK'L'-MIRZA. Camomile flowers.
p. *babooneh gáw:* بابونه گاو

(46) اخروت AKH-ROWT. अखरोट Walnut.
جوز چارمغز گردگان
a. *jowz.* p. *char mughz.* and *geer di-gán.*

(47) اخگر ÁK-GIR. A live coal.
अंगारा انگشت افروخته
h. *an-gá-rá* p. *unkisht áfrokhteh*

(48) اخينوس EKHEENOOS. Wild wheat.

(49) اخريط EKHREET. Wild leek.
बनकागंदना كندناي بري
h. *bun-ká gun-de-ná.* p. *gun-dé-ná bur-ree.*

(50) اخيل UKH-YUL. Name of a bird, whom the Arabians consider to be unlucky.

(51) اخزم UKH-ZUM. A young snake.
p. *már*

p. *már now.* مارنو

(52) اخيون UKH-YOON. *a.* Snake's head; name of a plant.

p. *rás ul úf-e-iy.* راس الافعي

(53) اخبروسه UKH BÉ-RU-SEH. Wild wheat.

बनगेहॊ دوسر كندم دشتي

h. *bun-gee-hoon.* v. p. *du-fir.* p. *gundum deshtee.*

(54) ادادا A-DÁ-DÁ. A species of mezereon.

p. *derukht kerem dáneh.* درخت کرم دانه

(55) آدا ÁDÁ. Green ginger.

अदरक आदा زنجبيل تر

h. *ád-ruck.* p. *zinjebeel tur.*

(56) ادرک ID-RICK. *a.* A small plum.

p. *áloo-cheh.* الوچه

(57) ادچاره U-DE-CHÁ-REH. The inverted thorn.

चिचिरा خاروازكون

v. h. *chee-ché-rá.* p. *khár wagzoon.*

(58) اداراقي Á-DÁ-RÁ-KEE. *sy.* Name of a bitter root, very hard when dry.

कुचला فلوس ماهي

h. *kootchelá.* p. *fe-loos máhee.*

(59) آذان الارنب AZÁN UL-ER-NUB. *a.* Hares' ears. A species of ribwort.

p. *we-rek bár-tung.* ورق بارتنک

(60) آذان الدب AZÁN ÚL DUB. *a.* Mullein. *p. goosh khyrs*, or bear's ears. كوش خرس

(61) آذان العبد AZÁN UL UBD. A species of shepherd's staff.

(62) آذان الفار AZÁN UL FAR. *a.* Mouse ear. p. *merjan goosh.* مرزانكوش

qu. hot and dry 2. *d.* half a direm.

(63) اذخر IZ-KEER. *a.* Camel's hay.

गंधबेल كاه مكي & كوركيا

h. *gund beyl.* p. *gowr-gee-á*, and *ká-muck-ee.*

(64) آذرياس ÁZREE-YASS. Gum of wild rue. صمغ سداب كوهي

p. *semegh sudáb kou-hee.*

(65) آذان القيس AZÁN UL KÉ-SEES. *a.* A species of house-leek.

(66) اذناب الخيل UZNÁB UL KYEL. *a.* The plant horse tail.

सिरसकागाछ

h. *see-rs ká gátch.* p. *ás-lunj.*

(67) آذان الفيل ÁZÁN UL FEEL. *a.* Drangwort.

p. *pulgoosh*, and *loof.* پيلكوش — لوف

(68) آذان الغزال AZÁN UL GHÉZÁL. *a.* A ſpecies of bugloſs.

(69) آذارافيون AZÁR-Á-FYOON. A ſpecies of foam of the ſea.

(70) آذريون AZREEYOON. According to ſome, the anemone; others ſay it is the camomile plant.

(71) آذريو AZIR-YOU. The ſunflower.

(72) آذان الجدي AZÁN UL JEDEE. *a.* Ribwort, arnogloſſa.

p. *liſſan ul heml.* لسان الحمل

(73) ارطاماسيا ÁRTE-MA-SY-Á. Artemeſia, mugwort.

p. *bir-un-ja-ſif.* برنجاسف

(74) ارسطا ÁRIS-TÁ. Henbane.

p. *bung.* بنك

(75) ارسطلوخيا ARISTÁLOOKHEEÁ. Long birthwort.

p. *zerewend teweel.* زراوند طويل

(76) ارمينا URMEENÁ. Sal ammoniac. p. *nowſhádir.* نوشادر

(77) آراتوا ÁRÁ-KOO-WÁ. A weed that grows amongſt wheat.

किका سهك كندم

p. *ſébuck gundum.* h. *keekd.*

(78) اروسا E-RU-SA. अरोसा & वांसा An Indian plant, called alſo *bunſá.*

(79) ارقب ER-KUB. The mountain goat. p. *búz kou-hee.* بزكوهي

(80) ارزت IR-ZUT. A ſpecies of fir.

p. *ſe-no-bér bey bir.* درخت صنوبر بي بر

The fir that does not bear fruit.

(81) اريد بريد Á-REED-BÁ-REED. A root which reſembles a ſplit onion. It is a native of *Seiſtan.*

(82) ارشد UR-SHUD. The marcaſite ſtone.

v. *mir-ká-ſhee-ſhá.* مرقشيشا

qu. hot and dry 2.

(83) ارثد UR-SUD. The chaſte tree.

संमालु پنجنكشت

p. *punjun gooſht.* h. *ſumbháloo.*

(84) ارند A-RUND. अरंड palma chriſti. p. *beed injeer.* بيدانجير

(85) ارز ÁRUZ. Rice.

चावल h. *chá-wul.* p. *be-renj.* برنج

(86)

(86) ارزيز UR-ZEEZ. *p.* Tin.

रांगा قلعی رصاص

h. *rán-gá.* v. *ku-lie.* a. *re-ſúſs.*

(87) ارماط UR-MAT. Name of a flower.

कैवरेकाफुल h. *kew-rĕh ká ſ'hool.*

(88) ارقط UR-KUT. The leopard.

p. *pe-lung.* پلنك

(89) ارماك UR-MÁK. Name of a tree.

कैवरेकागाच h. *kew-reh ká gátch.*

(90) اراك UR-ÁK. *a.* A tree, of whoſe roots are made tooth-picks.

पिलुकागाच h. *pe-loo ká gátch.*

qu. hot and dry, 1.—*prop.* deobſtruent.—*ch.* fragrant.—*d.* of the fruit 1 miſkál.

(91) ارمال رومي UR-MÁL ROOMEE. An aromatic bark of a tree growing in Yemen.

(92) اردم رومي UR-DUM-ROOMEE. The anemone.

v. *ázree-yoon.* آذريون

(93) ارقم URKUM. A ſnake, black and white. p. *mar ubluck.* مارابلق

(94) ارمانيقون UR-MÁ-NEE-KOON. Henbane ſeed.

p. *buz-ir ul bunj.* بزرالبنج

(95) ارقان UR-KÁN. A ſpecies of privet.

मिंदी h. *mhindee.* v. p. *hennah.* حنا

(96) اردشيران UR-DE-SHEERAN. A tree reſembling jaſmine.

(97) اربيان UR-BEE-YAN. A ſhrimp.

झींगा ملخ درياي

h. *jhingá.* p. *melekh de ry-á-i.*

(98) ارجان UR-JÁN. Wild almond.

जंगलीबादाम بادام كوهي

h. *jungelee bá-dám.* p. *bá-dám kou-hee.*

(99) ارجوان UR-JOO-WÁN. A tree bearing a beautiful purple flower.

p. *ur-ghé-wán.* ارغوان

qu. cold and dry.

(100) ارمنين UR-ME-NEEN. Wild pomegranate.

जंगलीअनार انار دشتي تلقل

h. *jungelee ánár.* a. *kilkul.* p. *ánár deſhtee.*

(101) ارسانيقون UR-SA-NEE-KOON. Yellow orpiment.

हरताल زرنيخ زرد

h. *hir-tál.* p. *zir-neikh zird.*

(102)

(102) ارسقیلون UR-SE-KE-LOON. The ſame.

(103) ارزن ÁR-ZUN. A kind of millet. चिना h. *chey-ná*.

(104) اراه Á-RÁH. Gum maſtich.

(105) ارجيقنه UR-JEE-KE-NEH. A yellow graſs uſed in dying.

असेपनक زرير

h. *as-pe-ruck*. p. *zé-reer*.

(106) اردفناني IR-UD-FE-NÁ-NEE. *v*. Wild cucumber.

(107) ارنبري UR-NUB-BIR-REE. The hare. ससा خركوش

h. *ſúſſá*. p. *khur-gooſh*.

(108) ارنب بحري UR-NUB BEH-REE. The ſea hare, a poiſonous fiſh, reſembling a ſhell.

(109) ارطي IR-TEE. The white poplar. v. *ſepeid-ár*. سپيدار

(110) ارغاموني UR-GHÁ-MOO-NEE. A flower reſembling the anemone.

(111) ازورد UZ-WIRD. The lote tree.

(112) اسموسا US-MOO-SÁ. Wild carrot.

(113) اسطرخا US-TIR-KHÁ. Red orpiment. मैन्सल زرنيخ سرخ

h. *mynſul*. p. *zir-neikh ſoorkh*.

(114) اسپند ISS-PUND. Seed of wild rue. v. *hir-mul*. حرمل

(115) استهخرما US-TEH KHURMA. Date ſtone.

prop. when burnt, it is drawing and detergent.

(116) اسرب US-RUB. A Lead.

(117) اسفيداج IS-FEE-DÁJ. White lead.

(118) اسغلنج IS-FE-LUNJ. The ſhrub horſe tail, or goat's beard.

(119) اسفنج IS-FUNJ. Sponge.

मुवाबादल ابرمرده

h. *moowa-bá-dul*. p. *abir-moordeh*.

(120) اسرنج IS-RINJ. Red lead.

संदोर h. *ſeindur*.

prop. drying. *ch*. a bright red. *ſuc*. white lead.

(121) اسفاناج IS-FÁ-NÁJ. Spinnage.

सागपालक اسپاناج

h. *ſág pá-luck*. p. *is-pá-náj*.

prop. cool and emollient. *cor*. pepper. *ſuc*. long cucumber; and purſlain.

(122) اسودسالخ US-WUD SÁ-LIKH. A black ſnake.

कालानाग

कालानाग مارسیاه
h. *kállá nág.* p. *már sy-ah.*

(123) اسفندسفید IS-FUND-SE-FEID. A ſpecies of muſtard-ſeed.

इसबंद تخم سپندان
h. *is-bund.* p. *tokhum-ſe-pen-dán.*

prop. anodyne.

(124) اسد USSUD. The lion.

बाघ h. *bgáh.* p. *ſheer.* شیر

(125) استهول کند IS-THOOL-KUND. अस्थोलकंद An Indian root.

(126) اسقنقور ISS-KUN-KOOR. The ſhink.

रितमछली ریگ ماهي نهنگ دشتي
h. *reyt mutch-lee.* p. *reig mábee,* and *ne-heng deſh-tee.* v. *ſé-kunkoor.* سقنقور

(127) اسمار IS-MÁR. Myrtle.

(128) اسطوخودوس US-TOO-KOO-DOOS. Stoechas.

(129) اسیوس US-YOOS. Fixt alkaline ſalt. h. *cheen ka loon.* चीनकालोन

(130) اسفیوس ISS-FÉ-YOOS. Seed of fleawort.

(131) اسقاقس ISS-KA-KIS. A ſpecies of millet.

(132) اسقولوس US-KOO-LOOS. A plant, whoſe root is very viſcous.

घाससरस گیاه سریشم
h. *gá-hſs ſir-eyſs.* p. *gee-áh ſir-ey-ſhum.*

(133) استطلس ISS-TUT-LUS. Jew's pitch.

(134) اسقوریدوس US-KOO-REE-DOOS. Rennet in general.

انفخه پنیرمایه
v. *un-fe-keh.* p. *pu-neer-máyeh.*

(135) اسطرماطوس US-TIR-MÁ-TOOS. Wild rue. اسپند

(136) اسد الارض USSUD UL URZ. The chameleon.

गरगिट حربا بوقلمون
h. *geer-git.* p. *boo-ke-le-moon.* v. *hir-bá.*

The chymiſts give this name alſo to quickſilver, on account of its aſſuming ſo many forms.

(137) استرنگ US-TRUNG. Mandrake.

लछमनालछमनी یبروح p. مردم گیا
h. *luckmun-á luck-mu-nee.* v. *yeb-rooj.* p. *mir-dum gee-á.*

(138) اسپرک AS-PE-RUCK. Melilot.

असपरक

(139) اسقیل IS-KEEL. Squill.

कांदा *kándá.* *peyáz deſhtee.* پیازدشتي

(140) اسفرم IS-FE-REM. Myrtle.

(141) اسقولوقندريون US-KOO-LOO-KOON-DIR-YOON. Spleenwort.

(142) اسارون Á-SÁ-ROON. Asarabaca. तगर h. *tuckir.*

(143) اسقورون US-KOO-ROON. Rust of iron.

خبث الحديد ريم اهن

a. *khubs'l' hé-deed.* p. *reem á-hun.*

किट h. *keeth.*

(144) اسطفلين IS-TUF-LEEN. Carrot.

p. *zir-duck.* زردک h. *gá-jir.* गाजर

(145) اسفيداج الجصاصين IS-FEY-DÉJ'L'JUSSA-SEEN. Shell lime.

कली اهک صدف

h. *kullee.* p. *á-huck sud-ef.*

(146) اسقيدوليون US-KEE-DOO-LE-YOON. Winter cherry.

(147) اسران ÁSS-RÁN. Milk curds.

(148) آس بنکه ÁSS-BIN-KEH. Myrtle.

(149) اسکنده US-GUN-DEH. असगंद An Indian plant.

It is heating, and stimulant.

(150) اسروره US-RÚ-REH. Indian spikenard.

v. *sem-bel ut teib.* سنبل الطيب

(151) اسخاره رومي ISS-KHÁ-REH-ROOMEE. A thorny grass.

(152) آس بري ÁSS BIR-REE. Wild myrtle.

(153) اشموسا & اسموسا USH-MOO-SA and US-MOO-SA. A species of merow.

(154) اشياف ماميسا Á-SHEYÁF MÁ-MY-SÁ. The juice of a species of poppy.

(155) اشنازداود USH-NÁZ DÁ-OUD. Dry hyssop; *vide* زوفا *zoofá.*

(156) اشترغار USH-TUR-GHÁR. Camel's thistle.

(157) اشتاليوس ISH-TE-LÁ-YOOS. An aromatic bark.

v. *dár-shee-shán.* دارشيشغان

(158) اشراش ISH-RÁSS. A plant, of which is made a very strong glue.

सरेस سريشم

h. *sir-eys.* p. *sir-ey-shem.*

(159) اشخيص ISH-KHEES. A species of mezereon.

(160) اشق USHUCK. Gum ammoniac.

صمغ

صمغ طراتیث صمغ بل شیرین

p. *se-mugh te-rá-tees*, and *se-mugh bil she-reen.*

(161) اشقاقل ISH-KÁ-KUL. Wild carrot.

(162) اشکیل چشم USH-KYL CHESH UM. A species of bramble.

v. *owsuj.* عوسج

(163) اشنان USH-NÁN. Glasswort.

चुक & चुबकशाय: غاسول

h. *chook.* & *chu-buck show-yeh.* p. *ghá-ful,*

qu. hot and dry 2. *prop.* detergent and caustic. *ch.* the best grows at Bark near Cufah, and is of a light green. *d.* half a direm. *cor.* poppy. *suc.* soap.

(164) آش بچکان ÁSH BUTCHE-GÁN. Castor.

(165) اشنه USH-NEH. Moss that grows in trees.

छरीला دواله

h. *cheree-lá.* p. *de-wá-leh.*

(166) اصل الهندبا USS'LÚL HIN-DU-BA. Root of succory.

(167) اصل العرطنیثا USS'LUL UR-TE-NY-SÁ. Root of arthenita, or sowbread. بخور مریم

(168) اصل الغرب USS'LU'L GHERB. Root of the mountain pine.

qu. hot and dry 2.

(169) اصل القصب USS'LU'L KUS-SEB. Root of the reed.

qu. hot and dry 2.

(170) اصل الذرت USSUL'Z' ZURT. Root of a species of millet.

p. *beykh jew-ár.* بیخ جوار

qu. cold and dry. *prop.* narcotic.

(171) اصابع الفتیات Á-SÁBA-UL-FE-TÉ-YAT. Sweet basil.

तुलसी انکشت کنیزکان

h. *tu'lsee.* p. *ungoosht kun-ee-zuck-án.*

(172) اصل الرازیانج USSUL 'UR RA-ZEE-Á-NUJ. Root of a species of anise.

सन्फकिजर بیخ بادیان

h. *sownf key jir.* p. *beykh bá-dy-án.*

(173) اصل اللفاح USSUL UL LOO-FAH. Mandrake root.

(174) اصل الجاوشیر USSUL UL JE-WÁ-SHEER. Root of the opoponax tree.

p. *beykh gáwsheer.* بیخ کاوشیر

(175) اصل الکبر USSUL UL KUB-IR. Root of the caper bush. بیخ کبر

p. *bekyh kobir.*

(176)

(176) اصل المر USSUL 'L' MÚRR. Root of the myrrh tree.

p. *beykh múrr.* بيخ مر

qu. hot and dry 2.

(177) اصل اللوز المر USSUL UL LOWZ UL MÚRR. Root of the bitter almond tree.

करुएबादामकीजर بيخ بادام تلخ

h. *ke-ru-ey bádám key jír.* p. *beykh bádám telkh.*

(178) اصابع صفر ÁSÁ-BÁ-SIFR. A root. p. *kuf me-riem.* كف مريم

It is of a dark yellow colour, and accounted good in curing the bite of any animal.

(179) اصابع هرمس ÁSÁ-BÁ HOOR-MUS. Hermodactyls.

p. *soorinján.* كل سورنجان

(180) اصل السوس USSUL US' SOOS. Liquorice root.

जीठीमद and मुलहटी بيخ مهك

h. *mooh-luttee*, and *jet-hee-mudh.* p. *beykh mé-huck.*

(181) اصل الكرفس USSUL UL KEREFS. Parsley root.

अजमुदकीजर بيخ كرفس

h. *uj-mood-key jír.* p. *beykh kerefs.*

(182) اصل السوسن الابيض USSUL' US' SO-SUN UL UBYEEZ. Root of white lily.

p. *beykh so-sun se-feid.* بيخ سوسن سفيد

(183) اصل اللوف USSUL UL LOOF. Root of dragonwort.

p. *beykh peel-goosh.* بيخ پيلگوش

qu. hot and dry, 3.

(184) اصل الاصف USSUL UL Á-SUF. Root of the caper bush; *vide* No. 175.

(185) اصطرك US-TE-RUCK. Storax.

qu. hot and dry. *cor.* coriander seed. *suc.* costus.

(186) اصل التنبول USSUL UT TUM-BOOL. Root of the betel plant.

कुलींजन بيخ پان

h. *ko-lin-jen.* p. *beykh pán.*

(187) اصل الفلفل USSUL UL FIL-FIL. Root of the long pepper shrub.

(188) اصل النيل USSUL UL NEEL. Root of *neel.*

p. *beykh hub ul neel.* بيخ حب النيل

The *neel* tree bears a purgative berry, called in Arabic *hub ul neel.*

(189) اصل الراسن USSUL UL RÁ-SUN. Root of elecampane.

بيخ زنجبيل شامي

p. *beykh zunjé-beel shámee.*

qu.

qu. hot and dry, 2.

(190) اصل فنطافلون USSUL FIN-TÁ-FE-LOON. Root of cinquefoil.

p. *beykh punjungoosht.* بيخ پنج انشكت

qu. hot and dry, 2.

(191) اصطفين IS-TÉ-FEEN. Carrot.

(192) اصول الاربعه USSOOL UL ÁR-BÁ-Á. The four roots, *viz.* fuccory, fennel, caper, and tamarisk.

(193) اصل الكثاه USS UL KUSS-ÁH. Parsley root.

(194) اصابع الغذاري ASÁ BA UL GHÉ-ZÁ-REE. A species of black grapes. कालीदाख انكور زيتوني

h. *ká-lee dákh.* p. *uugoor zietoonee.*

qu. hot and dry.

(195) اصل المازريون USSUL 'L' MÁZ-RI-YOON. Mezereon root.

p. *beykh must-roo.* بيخ مسترو

qu. hot and dry, 3.

(196) اصل النيلوفر الهندي USSUL NEE-LU-FIR HINDEE. Root of water lily.

कवलकीजर h. *konwul key jir.*

بيخ نيلوفر هندي p. *beykh nee-lu-fir-hindee.*

197) اصل السوسن السمان جوني USSUL US SO-SUN UL ASSMÁN JOO-NEE. Root of iris.

v. *jyrsá.* ايرسا

(198) اصل الخنثي USSUL'L'KHUN-SÁ. A glutinous root of a species of grass. p. *beykh gee-há. sé-rey-shum.* بيخ كياه سريشم

(199) اصل الانجدان الخراساني US-SUL'L'UN-JÉ-DÁN-UL- KHORÁ-SÁNEE. Root of a species of thistle.

(200) اضراص الكلب UZRÁSS UL KELB. Polypody.

(201) اضموط UZMOOT. A kind of filbert.

(202) اطميسا UT-MEE-SÁ. Mugwort.

(203) اطاء E-TÁ-Á. The white poplar. *vide* 109.

(204) اطريفل IT-REE-FUL. General name for myrobalans.

(205) اطراف زيتون UT-RÁF ZIE-TOON. Olive branches.

p. *shákh-há zietoon.* شاخهاي زيتون

(206) اطريه UT-RY-EH. A kind of vermicelli.

सिवै حلواي رشته
h. *ſeen-wi-ey.* p. *hul-wa-iy riſhteh.*

(207) اطباء الكبه UT-BÁ UL KEL-BEH. Sebeſtens.

(208) اظفار الطيب UZFÁR UT TEJB. Perfumed nails.

(209) اعين السراطين AI-YUN US SERÁTEEN. Seed of agnus caſtus.

vide 35.

(210) اغبر UGBAR. A Collyrium.

It is compoſed of wormſeed, tutty, and ſugar candy.

(211) اغيرس Á-GHEE-RIS. Walnut.

vide 46.

(212) اغيس Á-GHEES. One of the many names for agnus caſtus.

(213) اغرسطس UGHER-SE-TIS. A ſpecies of thiſtle.

v. *ſeel.* سيل p. *beyd gee-á.* بيد گيا

(214) اغلقه UGH-LEE-KEH. Syrup of grapes, dates, &c.

p. *dúſhab.* دوشاب

(215) اغالوجي ÁGHÁ-LOO-CHEE. Lignum aloes.

अगर h. *ugir.* p. *oud.* عود

(216) آفتاب پرست ÁF-TÁB PE-RUST. Worſhipper of the ſun.

This appellation is given to the ſunflower, the neelufir, and the chameleon.

(217) افشرج UF-SHÚ-REJ. Expreſſed juice.

افشرده and عصاره

p. *uf-ſhoor-deh*, and *uſſá-reh.*

(218) افرهنج UFRE-HUNJ. The herb curſuta.

p. *ku-ſhoos.* كشوث

(219) افكار UF-KÁR. Sneezewort.

नखछेकनी h. *nuck chee-ké nee.*

(220) افرنجمشك ÁFRUNJ-MISHK. A ſpecies of ſweet baſil.

तुलसी بالنكوي خورد

h. *túlſee.* p. *bá-lun-goo-ee-khoord.*

qu. hot and dry, 2. *cor.* violets. *ſuc.* cloves.

(221) افاسون ÁFÁ-SOON. Oil of radiſh.

मुलीकातिल روغن ترب

h. *moo-lee ká teil.* p. *roghen toorb.*

(222) افلاطون ÁFLÁ-TOON. Gum bdellium.

गुगल h. *goo-gul.* p. *mo-kul.* مقل

(223) افربيون E-FIR-BE-YOON. Euphorbium.

सिहंदकादुद شير درخت زقوم & فرفيون

h. *ſe-hoond ká doodh.* p. *ſheer derukht zuckoom.* v. *fir-fi-yoon.*

It is the milky juice of a prickly plant, called *Zuckoom*, &c.

(224) افسنتين UFSUNTEEN. Wormwood.

मसतारु برنجاسف كوهي

h. *muſ-tá-roo.* p. *burunja'-ſif kouhee.*

qu. hot and dry, 3. *prop.* deobſtruent and purgative, and deſtroying worms.

(225) افيلون UFYLOON. Mountain wormſeed.

درمنه كوهي p. *dir-me-neh kou-hee.*

(226) افيون UF-YOON. Opium.

अफीम شير خشخاش

h. *uf-eem.* p. *ſheer khuſh káſh.*

qu. cold, 4. dry, 3. *prop.* narcotic and ſedative. *ch.* that which diſſolves readily in water, and melts when expoſed to the ſun. *d.* The weight of a pea; for outward application, twice that quantity. *cor.* pepper, cinnamon, ſagapenum, parſley ſeed, and caſtor. *ſuc.* three times the weight, of henbane ſeed, with one-third more of the fruit of mandrake.

(227) افتيمون ÁFTEEMOON. Dodder of thyme.

आकासबेल h. *ákaſs beyl.*

(228) اناديه AFÁ-DY-AH. Heating medicines, ſuch as cloves, galangal, cinnamon, &c.

(229) افلنجه IF-LUN-JEH. A ſeed, reſembling muſtard, but of a fragrant ſmell.

p. *fe-lun-jeh.* فلنجه

It is chiefly uſed in perfumes.

(230) افعي UF-IEY. Snake, in general.

सांप h. *ſámp.* p. *mar.* مار

qu. hot and dry, 4. *prop.* attenuant. *ch.* a female. *d.* of the fleſh, three miſkáls. *cor.* Teriac or Venice treacle.

(231) اقاقيا Á-KÁ-KYÁ. Acacia.

(232) اقليميا EKLEE-MYA. The droſs of gold or ſilver.

prop. drying. *cor.* oil of almonds.

(233) اقسوس UK-SOOS. A ſmall viſcous berry.

(234) اقط U-KIT. Dried milk curds.

qu. cold and dry.

(235) اقحوان OKH-HYWÁN. Camomile flowers.

p. *báboonéh gáw.* بابونه گاو

(236) اقويلاسمون رومي ÁKOO-YEELÁ-SEMOON-ROOMEE. Balſam of Gilead.

p. *rogken bulſán.* روغن بلسان

(237) اقارون A-KÁ-ROON. Sweet flag.

p. *wuj.* وج

(238) اقطن يمني UKTIN YEMENEE. A ſpecies of vetch.

p. *bé-noo-máſh.*

p. *bé-noo-másh.* بنوماش

(239) اقومالي EKOO-MÁ-LEE. A mixture of honey and water.

(240) اقطي UK-TEE. The elder tree.

(241) اقطنالوقي UKTENÁ-LOO-KEE. A kind of white thorn.

दे माबा بادآورد

h. *deb-má-bá.* p. *bád-á-wird.*

(242) اكتمكت UK-IT-MUCKIT. The eagle stone.

करनजुवा خايه ابليس

h. *kerun-jewd.* p. *kha-yeb eblees.*

Suppofed to affift women in labour.

(243) اكشوث UKH-SHOOS. A fpecies of dodder.

(244) اكج UK-UJ. The medlar.

(245) اكر IG-IR. Sweet-fcented flag.

(246) اكرفس UK-REFS. Parfley.

v. *kerefs.* كرفس

(247) اكروفس UK-RU-FUS. Walnut.

p. *jowz-roomee.* جوزرومي

(248) آك AG. Name of a milky tree.

आग شجرعشر

a. *fhejer úfhir.*

(249) اكروهك UK-ROO-HUCK. Sarcocolla; *vide* No.

(250) اكليل الملك EKLEEL'UL MELIC. Melilot.

असपरक كياه قيصر زرير

h. *áf-pe-ruck.* p. *gee-áh ky-fir*, alfo *zereer.* vide 141.

(251) اكليل اهوض EKLEEL AHWUZ. Seed of an Indian plant.

अतंगनकिबीज h. *u-tun-gun kay beedj.*

(252) اكموبزان UK'MOÓ-YE-ZAN. A fpecies of pea.

(253) اكارىقون ÁKÁ-REE-KOON. Stone of the wild olive.

(254) اكل نفسه U-KEIL NEFSEH. Euphorbium.

v. *fir-fy-oon.* فرفيون

(255) اكاهولي AKÁ-HOO-LEE. An Indian plant.

अकाहुली

It is ufed in the cafe of the gonorrhœa.

(256) السا ULSA. A fpecies of anifeed..

(257) الب IL-IB. Aloes; *vide* 34.

(258) الوج Á-LOOJ. A plant, confidered as an antidote.

p. *gáz-ruck.* كازرك

(259) السنة العصافير UL-SINETUL ÁSÁ-

ÁSÁ-FEER. Sparrow's tongue, a ſeed.
इंदरजव اهر لسان العصافير
h. *inderjoe.* a. *liſſán us áſá-feer.* p. *ábir.*

(260) الماس UL-MÁSS. Diamond.
हिरा h. *bee-rá.* p. *máſs.* ماس

(261) البانيس UL-BÁ-NEES. A pot-herb. सागचौलाये h. *ſág chowlie.*

(262) البطوط ELIB-TOOT. A ſpecies of creeper.

(263) الطاروميي UL-UT-ROOMEE. A ſpecies of mint. p. *ſec-ſubr.* سيسبر

(264) الانيون UL-Á--NEE-YOON. Elecampane.

(265) اليو UL-YOU. Adam's fig; *vide.* 320.

(266) اليه UL-YE-ÁH. Tail of the Perſian ſheep.
दंबिके पुंछ دمدنبه
h. *dumbeyh key poontch.* p. *dúm dúmbeh.*
qu. hot and moiſt. *prop.* emollient.

(267) اله É-LÚK. The eagle.
p. *o-káb.* عقاب

(268) الاطيني A-LÁ-TEE-NEE. Fluellin.

(269) الايچي E-LA-IY-CHEE. इलाची Cardamum ſeed.

(270) السي ULSEE. अलसी Linſeed.

(271) امرا ÁM-RÁ. आमरा An Indian fruit, in ſhape reſembling the mangoe.

(272) امل بينت ÁMUL BEYNT. अमलबिंत An Indian fruit.

(273) آملج ÁM-LUJ. Emblic myrobalans.
आंवरा h. *aunwerá.* p. *á-mu-leh.* آمله

(274) امرود UMROOD. Pear p. *náſhpátee.* ناشپاتي

(275) اموس Á-MOOS. Biſhop's weed, ammi.

(276) امعاءالارض Á-MÁÁ UL URZ. Earthworm.

(277) امعاسين U-MÁ-SEEN. Juice of grapes.
दाककापानी آب غوره انگور
h. *dakh káy pá-nee.* p. *áb ghowrá ungoor.*

(278) امامون A-MA-MOON. Amomum.

(279) ام غيلان UM GHEELÁN. The gum-arabic tree. *vide* 414.

prop. astringent., and drying. *d. ad libitum.* *cor.* violets.

(280) انغطينا UN-FÉ-TEE-NÁ. *sy.* Wild rose.

(281) اناركيوا Á-NAR-GEE-WÁ. Poppy.

(282) انساسا UN-SÁ-SÁ. Raisins.

(283) انجسا UN-JEY-SÁ. A species of bugloss. v. p. *shunkár.* شنكار

(284) انقرديا UN-KIR-DYÁ. Anacardium.

(285) انوميا UN-OO-MY-Á Anemone.

(286) انطونيا UN-TOO-NY-Á. Endive.

(287) انتلهسودا UN-TE-LEH-SOWDÁ. Zedoary. *vide.* 412.

(288) انكورشغا UNGOOR SHÉ-FA. A species of nightshade.

(289) انب UN-UB. The egg plant. *vide* 382.

(290) انزروت UNZEROOT. Sarcocolla. p. *kun-ju-deh.* كنجده

(291) انجوج UNJOOJ. Lignum aloes. *vide* 216.

(292) انكور UNGOOR. Grapes. दाख h. *dákh.*

(293) انجير UNJEER. Fig. a. *teen.* تين

(294) انبرباريس UN-BER-BÁ-REES. Barberries.

(295) انجبارورومي UN-JE-BÁR ROOMEE. A plant growing on the banks of the Euphrates, used in stopping hemorrhages.

(296) اندر وطاقس UNDRYO-TÁ-KIS. a species of vetch.

(297) اناعيلس UNÁ-EEY-LUS. Marjoram.

(298) انفاق UNFÁK. Olive oil. p. *roghen zietoon.* روغن زيتون

(299) انجرك UNJERUCK. Marjoram.

(300) انجكك UNJOO-KUCK. A species of grain resembling pear-seed

(301) آنك Á-NUK. Lead.

(302) انجل UNJIL. Marsh-mallows.

(303) انفقون رومي UN-FU-KÚN-ROOMEE. A species of rose without smell.

सदागुलाब گل پياده h. *sud-*

h. *ſud-á goolâb.* p. *gool pé-yá deh.*

(304) انيسون Á-NEE-SOON. Aniſeed.

सोन्फ़ رازيانه رومي

h. *ſownf.* p. *rá-zy-á-neh roomee.*

(305) انجدان UN-JU-DAN. The aſafœtida plant.

हींग का रोख दرخت انكوزه

h. *hing ká rookh.* p. *dirukht un-goo-zeh.*

qu. hot and dry, 3. *prop.* deobſtruent, attenuant, and diaphoretic. *ch.* white. *d.* one direm. *cor.* vinegar. *ſuc.* the root thereof.

(306) اندراين IN-DE-RÁ-YEN. इंदरायन The fruit of the coloquintida plant. p. *hunzil.* حنظل

(307) انجن UNJUN. अंजन Collyrium in general.

(308) اندروخورون UNDEROO-KHU-ROON. A weed that grows amongſt wheat and barley, the ſeed of which is red, and very bitter.

(309) اندرجو INDIR-JOW. इंदरजव Sparrow's tongue. A ſeed. *vide* 261.

p. *liſſân ul us-á-feer.* لسان العصافير

(310) انجيده UN-JEE-DEH. Wild leek.

(311) انفحه UN-FÉ-KEH. Rennet in general. चुस्ताः پنيرمايه

h. *chuſtâb.* p. *pé-neer-má-yeh.*

qu. hot and dry, 2. *prop.* attenuant and deobſtruent. *ch.* that which has been ſqueezed quite dry. *cor.* honey.

(312) انفحة الارنب UN-FÉ KÉTUL URNEB. Rennet of a hare.

پنيرمايه خرگوش

p. *pé-neer-má-yeh khurgooſh.*

(313) انفحة الفرس UNFÉ KÉTÚL FERES. Rennet of a horſe.

(314) انفحة الخشف UNFÉ KÉ-T'UL KHI-SHIF. Rennet of a male kid of a mountain-goat, that is a firſtling.

(315) انفحة الجمل UN-FÉ-KÉ-TÚL JÉ-MÉL. Rennet of a camel.

(316) انفحة العجل UN-FE-KE-T'UL E-JIL. Rennet of a calf.

(317) انقطريون IN-KIT-REE-YOON. Amber.

(318) انكبين UN-GU-BEEN. Honey.

(319) انجره UN-JE-REH. Nettle.

चटंगन كزنه

h. *á-tun-gen.* p. *guz-neh.*

(320) انجيردشتي INJEER DÉSH-TEE. Adam's fig. *vide* 265.

v. *in-*

v. *injeer Adem.* انجيرادم

(321) انبوت الراعي UMBOOT'TR-RA-IY. A fpecies of Houfe-leek.

(322) انبوت ملكي UMBOOT MUL-E-KEE. The amaranth.

(323) انكمه UN-KÚ-MEH. The in-verted thorn.

(324) اناليقي رومي UN-Á-LEE-KEE-ROOMEE. Nettle.

(325) انبلي UMBLEE इंबली Ta-marind. p. *temr hindee.* تمرهندي

(326) اومادا OW-MÁ-DÁ. Expreffed juice of wild cucumber.

(327) اوكنج OW-KUNJ. Sebeftens.

(328) اوسپيد OWS-PEYD. A fpecies of water lily.

(329) اوذر OW-ZIR. Water. पानी h. *pá-nee.* a. *máá.* ماء p. *áb.* آب

(330) اوز OWZ. Water-fowl. *vide* 6.

(331) اونانيس OW-NÁ-NEES. Pomegranate buds.

p. *fhé-goo-feh á-nár.* شكوفه انار

(332) اوشع OW-SHÁ The marten, or fable. p. *fé-moor.* سمور

(333) اوداساليون OW-DÁ-SÁ LÍ-YOON. Wild Parfley.

p. *kerefs kou-hee.* كرفس كوهي

(334) اوقيمن OW-KY-MUN. Wild fweet bafil.

(335) اوقطاريون OW-KÉ-TÁ-RI-YOON. Hemp agrimony.

(336) اورمالي OWR-MÁ-LEE. Juice refembling honey, obtained from a certain tree, whofe name is not mentioned.

(337) اونومالي OW-NOO-MÁ-LEE. A mixture of honey and wine.

p. *fhé ráb wu affal.* شراب وعسل

(338) اهليلج اسود AH-LEE-LUJ US-WUD. Black myrobalans.

जंगीहर هليله سياه

h. *zun-gee har.* p. *he-lee-leh fee-áh.*

qu. cold 1, dry 2. *prop.* cathartic. *ch.* black. *d.* of the fkins 1 or 2 direms; in decoction 7 to 10 direms. *cor.* honey. *fuc.* chebulic myroba-lans.

(339) اهليلج اصفر AH-LEE-LUJ ASFIR. Yellow myrobalans.

हरतकी هليله زرد

h. *hirtuckee.* p. *hé-lee-leh zird.*

qu. cold 1, dry 2.—*prop.* cholagoga and tonic.—*ch.* plump. *d.* of the fkins as far as 5 direms; in decoction from 7 to 20 direms. *cor.* fugar-candy or manna, with jujubes.

(340) اهلال القسط AH-LÁL UL KOUST. A fpecies of fweet bafil.

(341)

(341) اهک Á-HUCK. Lime.

चुना h. *choo-ná.*

(342) اهليلج كابلي AH-LEE-LUJ CÁ-BULEE. Chebulic myrobalans.

अंबयाहर هليله كلان
h. *umbe-á-hér.* p. *he-lee-leh kelán.*

qu. cold and dry. *prop* melanagoga. *eb.* large and plump, and that will ſink in water. *d.* 5 to 10 direms. *cor.* honey. *ſuc.* black myrobalans.

(343) IYR-SÁ. Root of blue iris.

qu. hot and dry. *prop.* ſuppurative, and deobſtruent. *eb.* black and hard, full of knots, and fragrant. *d.* 2 direms. *cor.* honey.

(344) ايلوا EY-LEW-Á. ऐलवा Aloes. p. *ſyb-ir.* صبر

(345) اينكر IN GÚR. ईंगुर Vermilion. p. *ſhin-girf.* شنكرف

(346) ايدع رومي IY-DÁ-ROO-MEE. Dragon's blood.

(347) ايل EE-YUL. The mountain cow. p. *gaú kou hee.* كاوكوهي

(348) ايهقان IY-KU-KÁN. A ſpecies of lupin.

(349) ايرسون EER-SOON. Talc; *vide* 16.

(350) ايرون IY ROON. Yellow orpiment. p. *gow-gird zird.* كوكرد زرد

(351) ايرن IY-RUN. Milk curds. p. *dowgh.* دوغ

(352) ايغاقين EY-KÁ-KEIN. Lignum aloes. p. *owd.* عود

(353) ايرقان EER-KÁN. A ſpecies of privet. p. *henná.* حنا

(354) ايرفيون EER-FI-YOON. The violet.

ب

(355) باقلا BÁ-KÉ-LÁ. A ſpecies of bean.

qu. cold and dry, 2. *prop.* aſtringent.

(356) بالا BÁLÁ. बाला alſo KEN-DUL. कंडुल An odoriferous graſs.

It is uſed for tents and doors in the hot ſeaſon, and being kept wet, the wind in paſſing through is cooled from 120 to 76 degrees.

(357) باجرا BÁJ-RA. बाजरा A ſpecies of grain uſed for food.

(358) بانسا BANSA. बांसा alſo A-RUSÁ. अरुसा An Indian plant.

(359) پاڈرا PÁD-RÁ. पाडरा alſo PÁ-DUL. पाडल Flower of an Indian tree.

It is uſed as a perfume.

(360) پات PÁT. पात Raw silk, *vide* 20.

(361) بارِدست BÁR-DUST. Ebony. *vide* 12.

(362) بادنج BÁDNUJ. Cocoanut.

(363) بابونج BÁBOONUJ. Camomile flower.

qu. hot and dry. *prop.* attenuant, deobstruent, and discutient. *ch.* large yellow flower. *d.* a pugil. *cor.* honey, or oil of roses. *suc.* milolet, or mugwort.

(364) بادروج BÁD-ROOJ. A species of sweet basil.

जंगलीतोलसी ترہخراساني

h. *junglee tulsee.* p. *tur-eh khorásánee.*

qu. hot and dry. *prop.* deobstruent, cordial, styptic. *ch.* fresh and pungent. *d.* of the seed 2 direms. *suc.* tulsee.

(365) باداورد BÁ-DÁ-WÚRD. A prickly shrub.

जवास شوكةالبيضا

h. *jownwásá* a. *showkt ul'-by-zá.*

(366) بارود BÁ-RUD. Fixed alkali salt, natron. *vide* 129.

(367) باراهيكند BÁRA-HY-KUND. बाराहीकंद An Indian plant.

qu. hot and dry 1. *prop.* drying. *ch.* fresh, white leaves. *d.* one direm and a half. *cor.* wormwood. *suc.* fumitory.

(368) بارزد BÁR-ZUD. Galbanum.

बरीजा بيرزد قنه

h. *bir-ee-já.* p. *beer-zud.* v. *kunneh.*

qu. hot 3, dry 2. *ch.* soft, and yellow, like honey; pungent. *cor.* gum ammoniac. *suc.* sagapenum.

(369) پاكهانبهيد PÁ-KHEN-BHIED. पाखानबिद Gentian.

(370) پاكر PÁKIR पाकर An Indian fruit tree.

(371) پادزهر PÁD-ZEHR. Bezoar.

जहरमुहरः پايزهر

h. *zehr-moh-rir.* p. *pá-iy zehr.*

(372) بابوسر BÁ-BOO-SIR. Adulterated camphor.

(373) بابسر BA-BE-SIR. Another name for senna.

(374) بانس BÁNS. बांस Bamboo.

p. *ni-ee hin-dee.* ني هندي

qu. cold. *prop.* emollient.

(375) باروق BÁ-ROOK. Ceruse of tin, or of lead.

(376) پالك PÁ-LÚCK. Spinnage. *vide* 121.

(377) بايبرنك BÁ-IY BERENG. A grain resembling pepper.

qu. hot and dry.

(378) بالنك BÁ-LUNG. A species of citron, *vide* 7.

(378)

(379) بارتنک BAR-TUNG. Ribwort.

(380) بادام BÁ-DAM. Almond.

a. *lowz.* لوز

(381) پان PAN. पान Betel leaf.

p. *birg tumbowl.* برک تنبول

(382) بادنجان BÁD-IN-JAN. The egg plant. वैगुन बहंटा

h. *byn-gun* and *báhn-tá.*

(383) بان BÁN. The Persian lilac.

बकायन h. *buck-á yin.*

(384) بارسطاريون BÁR-IS-TAR-YOON. Vervain.

(385) باديان BÁDEE-YAN. *p.* A species of aniseed.

(386) بارو BÁROO, बारु also BÁ-LOO.

बालू Sand. p. *reyg.* ريک a. *reml.* رمل

(387) باتو BÁ-TOO. A purgative seed.

v. *dund.* دند जमालगोटा *jemál gowtá.*

(388) بادرنجبويه BÁD-RUNJ-BOO-YEH. A species of sweet basil.

h. *rám tulsee.*

(389) بالنکو BÁLUN-GOO. Another name for the above.

(390) بابوسه BÁ-BOO-SEH. The bud of any tree. कुन्पल h. *kown-pul.*

(391) بابله BA-BÚ-LEH. Liquid Storax.

(392) باخه BÁ-KHEH. The tortoise.

कछेवा سنک پشت

h. *kutch-be-wá.* p. *sung púsht.*

(393) بابونه BABOONEH. Camomile flowers.

(394) باقلاقبطي BÁ-KE-LA KIP-TEE. Egyptian lupin.

(395) باقلامصري BÁ-KÉ-LA MIS-REE. The same.

(396) باجي BAJEE. *h.* Nitre. *vide* 9.

(397) باباري BÁ-BÁ-REE. *sy.* Black pepper.

(398) بارهي BÁR-HEE, also NEER-BISSEE. Zedoary. बा नहि & नरबसी

v. *jedwar.* جدوار

(399) ببغا BUB-GHÁ. *a.* A parrot.

h. *tow-tá,* and *sew-a.* p. *too-tee.* طوطي

(400) ببول BA-BOOL. The gum arabic tree. p. *mugheelán.* مغيلان

(401) پتپاپرا PIT-PÁP-RÁ. पितपापरा Fumitory.

p. *sháhtereh.* شاهتره

(402) پتجيا PUT-JE-ÁY. पतजेया An Indian tree.

(403) بتهوا BUT-HEW-A. बतवा Orach.

(404) بجورا BE-JEW-RÁ. *b.* Citron. *vide* 30.

(405) بجربهانک BUJ-JIR BHANG. भांग Tobacco. v. *tumbá-coo.* تنباكو

qu. hot and dry 4. *prop.* narcotic, and deobstruent. *cor.* milk. In the appendix is an account when this plant was brought into Hindostan.

(406) بجم BOOJM. Fruit of the tamarisk.

माईन کزمازو ثمرةالطرفا

h. *má-een* p. *guz-má-zoo.* a. *sumrut ul-turfeh.*

(407) بخورمريم BÉ-KHOOR MIRIEM. Sowbread.

v. *shejereh miriem.* شجرهمريم

(408) بدليون BUD-LEE-YOON. *sy.* Bdellium.

गुगल h. *goo-gul.* مقل v. *mo-kul.*

(409) پدلون PUD-LOON. पदलौन Salt of bitumen.

p. *nemuck see-yah.* نمک سياه

(410) برهتيا BE-REH-TYÁ. बरेहतेया also BUDDES KUT-Á-IY बडेसकटैये An Indian prickly shrub.

(411) بر BURR. Wheat.

गेहें h. *geehoon.* p. *gundum.* گندم

(412) بر BIR. बर An Indian fruit-tree. a. *zát uz-ze-wánib.* ذاةالذوانب

(413) برنجاسف BIR-UN-JA-SIF. Mugwort. गंदमार h. *gund-már.*

ch. yellow. *cor.* aniseed.

(414) برقوق BIR-KOOK. Apricot.

खोबानी مشمش

h. *khoobá-nee.* p. *mishmish.*

(415) برواق BIR-WAK. The herb asphodel.

v. *gee-d-sir-eys.* كياهسريس

(416) برنجمشک BERUNJ-MISHK. A species of sweet basil. *vide* 364 & 388.

(417) بربال BIR-BÁL. बरबाल Coral. मूंगा بسد مرجان

h. *moongá.* a. *bussed.* p. *mirján.*

(418) برغول BIR-GHOWL. Wheat coarsely ground.

p. *de-lee-deh gundum.* دليدهگندم

(419) برتوم BIRTOOM. Dates well dried.

p. *khurmá-iy beeroon.* خرماي بيرون

(420) پرشوم PIR-SHOOM The reed.

(421) برم BURUM. Buds of the gum arabic tree.

(422) بردوسلام BURD-WU-SALAM. Ribwort. *vide* 379.

p. *wer-*

p. *weruck bartung.* ورق بارتنك

(423) برسن BEER-SOON. Cotton.

रुयै h. *rew-ey.* p. *poombeh.* پنبه

(424) پرسياوشان PIR-SY-OW-SHÁN. Maiden hair.

राजहंस h. *raj hunſs.*

qu. hot and dry. *ch.* dark red ſtalks with green leaves. *d.* three to ten direms. *ſuc.* violets, and root of liquorice.

(425) برنان BIR-NÁN. बरनान

A tree growing in Ajmeer, uſed for making roſaries.

(426) برشيان دارو PIR-SHE-YÁN DA-ROO. A pot-herb, of a red colour.

qu. cold, and dry. *ſuc.* nightſhade, or ribwort.

(427) برنج كابلي BIR-UNJ CÁBU-LEE. A grain reſembling poppy.

बाबरंग برنك

h. *bá-iy be-rung.* p. *berung.*

qu. hot and dry. *prop.* aſtringent, and *anthelmintic.* *ch.* ſmall, reddiſh. *d.* three to ten direms with new milk. *cor.* gum tragacanth. *ſuc.* Turkiſh lupins.

(428) بردي BIR-DEE. The Egyptian papyrus. पतीरा تك

h. *put-ee-rá.* p. *tuck.*

(429) برطانيقي BIR-TÉ-NEY-KEE. The flower called cockſcomb.

(430) بزرقطونا BUZIR KE-TOO-NÁ. Seed of fleawort. p. *uſ-pé-ghool.* اسپغول

qu. cold and moiſt. *prop.* diſcutient. *ch.* large, of a dark red, and that will ſink in water. *d.* two to three direms. *cor.* gum tragacanth. *ſuc.* quince ſeed.

(431) بزرالقثا BUZIR UL KIS-Á. Seed of a ſpecies of cucumber.

ककरीकेबीज تخم خيارزه

h. *kuckree key beej.* p. *tokhem khyar-zeh.*

qu. cold and moiſt. *ch.* large, and full. *cor.* oxymel. *ſuc.* cucumber ſeed.

(432) بزرالهندبا BUZIR ÚL HIN-DU-BÁ. Endive ſeed.

p. *tokhem káſ-nee.* تخم كاسني

qu. temperate. *ch.* cultivated, freſh, and full. *d.* two to three direms. *ſuc.* oxymel.

(433) بزربقلةالحمقا BUZIR BUCK LET ÚL HÚKÉ-MÁ. Purſlain ſeed.

लोनेयाकेबीज تخم تورك وخرنه

h. *loonyá key beej.* p. *tokhem túruck,* and *khereſeh.*

(434) بزرالسداب BUZIR US SUD-ÁB. Seed of rue.

qu. hot and dry. *ch.* black and large. *d.* one to two direms. *ſuc.* gum tragacanth.

(435) بزرالقنب BUZ-IR-UL KUN-NEB Hemp ſeed.

सनेकेबीज.

संकेबीज تخم بنک
h. *sun key beej.* p. *tokhem bung.*

(436) بزرالکرنب BUZ-IR-UL KIRNUB. Cabbage-seed.

p. *tokhem kullum.* تخم کلم

(437) بزرالشبت BUZR'US SHIBBET. Fennel seed.

सुयैकेबीज h. *sew-ay key beej.*

qu. hot and dry. *prop.* emetic, *d.* two direms. *cor.* honey.

(438) بزرللفت BUZ-IR UL LUFT. Turnip seed.

p. *tokhem shulghum.* تخم شلغم

qu. hot and moist. *ch.* large, and red. *d.* two direms. *cor.* melon seed.

(439) بزرالفنجنکشت BUZ-IR-UL FUNJUNGOOSHT. Seed of the agnus castus.

संभालुकेबीज h. *sumbhaloo key beej.*

qu. hot and dry. *ch.* large. *d.* two direms. *cor.* milk.

(440) بزرالکشوث BUZ-IR-UL KESHOOS. Seed of the plant cuscute.

अमरबिलकेबीज *um-er beyl key beej.*

d. two direms. *cor.* honey. *suc.* endive seed.

(441) بزرالکراث BUZ-IR-UL KURRÁSS. p. *tokhem gundná.* تخم گندنا

(442) بزرالبنج BUZ-IR-UL BUNJ. Black henbane-seed. *vide* 42.

ch. black *prop.* astringent, and styptic. *d.* one to two dangs. *cor.* honey. *suc.* opium.

(443) بزرالکاکنج BUZ-IR UL KAKNEJ. Seed of the Winter cherry.

تخم عروسک در پرده

p. *tokhem u-roosuck dir pirdeh.*

(444) بزرالرازیانج BUZ-IR-UL RÁZI-YÁ-NEJ. A species of aniseed.

सोंफ تخم بادیان
h. *sownf.* p. *tokhem badyán.*

(445) بزرالبطیخ BUZ-IR-UL BETEEKH. Musk-melon seed.

p. *tokhem khirboozeh.* تخم خربزه

qu. hot and moist. *prop.* when dry it is emetic. *d.* two to five direms. *cor.* honey.

(446) بزرالاسفناج BUZ-IR UL ISFANAJ. Spinnage seed. *vide* 121.

(447) بزرالرشاد BUZ-IR UL RESHÁD. Seed of garden cresses.

हालेम تخم تره تیزک
h. *he-lém.* p. *tokhem terreh tey-zuck.*

(448) بزرالقسد BUZ-IR-UL KUSUD. Cucumber seed.

खीरेकेबीज تخم خيار بالنك

h. *kee ray key beej.* p. *tokem khyár bálung.*

(149) بزرالورد BUZ-IR UL WURD.

Rose ſeed.

prop. aſtringent, and ſtyptic. *ch.* that of the Perſian roſe. *d.* 2 direms. *cor.* tragacanth.

(450) بزرالعصفر BUZ-IR UL US-FIR. Seed of ſafflower.

कुसुंभकेबीज خسک دانه

h. *kuſoombh key beej.* p. *khuſ-uck dáneh.*

(451) بزباز BUZ-BÁS. M ce.

जावत्री بسباسه

h. *jáw-itree.* v. *biſ-bá-ſeh.*

(452) بزرالخس BUZ-IR-UL KHUSS.

Lettuce ſeed.

p. *tokhem ká-hoo.* تخم كاهو

qu. cold and dry. *d.* one to two direms. *cor.* maſtich.

(453) بزربلاسقيس BUZ-IR-BUL-Á-SE-KEES. Seed of garden creſſes. *vide* 450.

(454) بزرالحماض BUZ-IR-UL HU-MAZ. Sorrel ſeed.

चुकेकेबीज تخم ترشه

h. *chewká key beej.* p. *tokhem tu'rſheh.*

qu. cold and dry. *ch.* of a reddiſh brown. *d.* two direms. *cor.* parſley ſeed, and aniſeed.

(455) بزرالمط BUZ-IR'UL MUT.

Seed of wild pomegranate.

p. *ánardaneh deſhtee.* انار دشتي

(456) بزرالسرمق BUZ-IR UL SIR-MUC. Seed of orach.

बतुवेकेबीज تخم قطف

h. *but-hoo-á key beej.* p. *tokhem kitf.*

(457) بزرالسلق BUZ-IR UL SULK.

Beet ſeed.

p. *tokhem chukundir.* تخم چقندر

(458) بزاق BU-ZAK. Saliva.

राल लार لعاب دهن

h. *ral,* alſo *lár.* p. *lu-db dehn.*

(459) بزرك BUZRUC. Linſeed.

p. *tokhem kut-án* تخم كتان *vide* 273. and 467.

(460) بزرالفجل BUZ-IR UL FUJL.

Radiſh ſeed.

मुलीकेबीज تخم ترب

h. *moolee key beej.* p. *tokhem toorb.*

qu. hot and dry. *prop.* emetic, and ſtimulent *d.* two direms. *cor.* coriander ſeed.

(461) بزرالسان الحمل BUZ-IR UL LISSAN UL HEML. Seed of Rib-wort. بارتنك p. *bartung.*

qu.

qu cold and dry. *ch.* of a reddish brown. *d.* three direms. *cor.* honey. *suc.* sorrel seed.

(462) بزرالبصل BUZ-IR-UL BUSSUL. p. *tokhem py-az.* تخم پیاز

qu. hot and dry. *d.* two direms.

(463) بزرالخمخم BUZ-IR UL KHOOMKHOOM. Seed of wild pomegranate. *vide* 458.

(464) بزرالكتان BUZ-IR-UL KUTÁN. Linseed. *vide* 462.

(465) بزرالنمام BUZ-IR-UL-NÁMÁN. Seed of mother of thyme.

बरनानकेबीज तخم سيسنبر

h. *bernàn key beej.* p. *tokhem see-sumber.*

ch. black. *d.* three direms. *cor.* gum tragacanth. *suc.* linseed.

(466) بزرالهليون BUZ-IR UL HULYOON.

नागदोनकेबीज تخم مارجوبه

h. *nag-done.* p. *tokhem már-chowbeh.*

qu. hot and moist. *d.* two direms. *cor.* honey.

(467) بزرالريحان BUZ-IR UL RYHAN. Sweet basil seed.

तोलसीकेबीज h. *tulsee key beej.*

qu. hot. *prop.* astringent. *d.* one miskál with cold water, or rose water. *cor.* sweet marjoram.

(468) بزرالمازريون BUZ-IR UL MÁZRI-YOON. Mezereon seed.

p. *tokhem must-ru.* تخم مسترو

prop. emetic.

(469) بزرالرطبه BUZ-IR UL RUTBEH. Seed of an odoriferous grass.

p. *tokhem aspist.* تخم اسپست

qu. hot and moist. *ch.* yellow. *suc.* turnip seed.

(470) بزرالخرفه BUZ-IR UL KIRFEH. Purslain seed.

लोनेयाकेबीज تخم تورك

h. *loony-àn key beej.* *tokhem tu-ruck.*

qu. cold, 3. *d.* in acute fevers, an infusion of five direms. *cor.* sugar candy. *suc.* seed of fleawort.

(471) بزرالهوه BUZ-IR UL HEEWEH. Seed of mallows.

p. *toodree.* تودري

(472) بزرالانجره BUZ-IR UL UNJEREH. Nettle seed.

अटंगकेबीज تخم كزنه

h. *utungen key beej.* p. *tokhem guzneh.*

qu. hot and dry. *d.* half a miskál to three direms. *suc.* seed of cresses.

(473) بزرالكرفس البستاني BUZ-IR UL KEREFS UL BOSTÁNEE. Garden parsley seed. *vide* 38.

(474) بزرالخبازي بزرالخطمي BUZ-IR ÚL KHUBÁZE, and BUZ-IR ÚL KHIT-

KHITMEE. Mallows, and marſh-mallows ſeed. *vide* 471.

ſuc. cucumber ſeed.

(475) بزرالرمان البري BUZ-IR UL RU-MAN UL BIR-REE. Seed of wild pomegranate.

(476) بزرالجزرالبستاني BUZ-IR UL JUZR'IL BOSTÁNEE. Garden carrot ſeed.

गाजर के बीज تخم زردك

h. *gá-jir key beej.* p. *tokhem zirduck.*

d. one direm.

(477) بزرالجزرالبري BUZ-IR UL JUZR'IL BIR-REE. Seed of wild carrot. تخم كزر صحراي

p. *tokhem guz-ir ſerá-iy.*

(478) بزرالحندقوقي BUZ-IR UL HUND-KOW-KEE. Seed of the lote tree.

ſuc. tares.

(479) بزرالرازيانج الرومي BUZ-IR UL RÁZEE-A-NEJ UL ROOMEE. Aniſeed. p. *aneeſoon.* انيسون

(480) پستا PISTÁ. पिसता Piſtachio nut. a. *fiſ-tuc.* فستق

(481) بستج BIS-TUJ. *a.* Frankincenſe. p. *koonder.* كندر

(482) بستيتاج رومي BUS-TEE-TÁJ. ROOMEE. A ſmall creeping plant.

गुखरु h. *gookehroo.* p. *khuſ-uck.* خسك

(483) بسفايج BUSFA-IJ. Polypody.

कंगाली h. *khungálee.*

(484) بسد BU-SUD. *a.* Coral. *vide* 417.

(485) بسر BU-SUR. Unripe dates.

(486) بستان افروز BOSTÁN UF-ROZE. The plant cockſcomb.

जटाधारी and कलगा تاج خروس

h. *je-tá-dáh-ree,* and *kulgá.* v. *táj khe-roos.*

qu. cold and dry. *prop.* aſtringent. *ch.* that which has been dried in the ſhade. *d.* two to four direms, or of the ſeed one miſkal. *cor.* frank-incenſe. *ſuc.* ſorrel.

(487) پستان سك PISTÁN SUG. *p.* Sebeſtens.

लसुरा h. *lehſoorá.* v. *ſepiſtán.* سپستان

(488) پستاجو PIST JOW. Barley meal. p. *árud jow.* اردجو

(489) بسباسه BUS-BÁ-SEH. Mace. *vide* 451.

(490) بشبش BUSH BUSH. Leaves of the coloquintida plant.

(491) بشترغ BUSH-TURUGH. Melilot. vide 250.

(492) بصل الذيب BUSSUL ÚZ' ZEEB. A species of wild onion.

v. *bulboos.* بلبوس

(493) بصاق القمر BU-SÁK-UL KUMR. The moon stone. Selenites.

v. a. *hejr ul kumr.* حجر القمر

(494) بصل الفار BUSSUL-UL-FÁR. Squills. vide 139.

(495) بصل النرجس BUSSUL-UL-NUR JIS. Root of the narcissus.

qu. hot and dry. *d.* two miskals for an emetic.

(496) بصاق BUSÁK. Saliva.

qu. hot and moist. *prop.* suppurative and deobstruent. *ch.* fasting.

(497) بصل العنصل BUSSUL-UL-UNSUL. Squill. vide 139.

(498) بصل BUSSUL. Onion.

पयाज h. *pee-áj.* p. *pee-yáz.* پياز

qu. hot and dry. *prop.* discutient and attenuant. *ch.* white. *d.* of the seed two direms. *cor.* vinegar.

(499) بطيخ BE-TEEKH. Musk melon. खरबुजः خربوزه

h. *khir-boozá.* p. *khir-boozeh.*

qu. hot and moist. *prop.* stimulant, diuretic, and detergent: the skin is emetic.

(500) بط BÚT. *p.* Goose

हंस h. *buns.* p. *káz.* قاز

(501) بطم BOOTM. The turpentine tree.

(502) بطيخ زقي BE-TEEKH ZIC-KEE. Water-melon.

तरबुज هندوانه

h. *turbooz.* p. *hindu-á-neh.*

qu. cold and moist. *ch.* sweet and juicy.

(503) بعر BÁR Globular dung of animals.

मंगनी h. *mig-nee.* p. *pishkel.* پشكل

prop. These are used in cataplasms.

(504) بق BUCK. Gnat.

मछर h. *much-hér.* p. *push-eh.* پشه

(505) بقر BUCKIR. Ox, bull, or cow.

गाय & बैल گاو

h. *byln,* and *gow.* p. *gáw.*

(506) بقلة الحمقا BUCKLUT'UL' HU-ME-KÁ. Purslain.

लुनियासाग تورك

h. *loonyá ság.* p. *tooruck.*

qu. cold and moist. *prop.* narcotic. *ch.* broad leaves. *cor.* parsley.

(507) بقلة الزهرا BUCKLÚTÚL ZEH-RÁ. The same.

(508) بقلة الضب BUCKLUT ÚZ-ZUB. A species of sweet basil.

p. *bá-*

p. *ba-lun-goo bir-ree.* بالنكوي بري

(509) بقلة العدس BUCKLUT ÚL' UD-US. Calamint.

p. *powd-neh birree.* پودنه بري

(510) بقلة الخطاطيف BUCKLUT ÚL KHE-TÁ-TEEF. Celadine.

(511) بقلة الملك BUCK LUT ÚL MELIC. Fumitory.

(512) بقلة الغزال BUCK LÚT ÚL GHEZÁL. Dittany.

(513) بقلة الفارستم BUCK LUT 'UL' FÁRISTUM. Balm.

p. *bádrunj bu-yeh.* بادرنجبويه

(514) بقلة الخراسانيه BUCK LUT UL KHORÁSANYEH. Sorrel.

(515) بقلة الاترجيه BUCKLUT 'UL' UT-RU-JY-EH. Balm.

(516) بقلة البارده BUCKLUTÚL BÁ-RE-DEH. Ivy.

p. *lubláb.* لبلاب

(517) بقلة الذهبيه BUCKLUT 'UZ' ZEH-BI-YEH. Spinnage. *vide* 121.

(518) بقلة المبارك BUCLÚT ÚL MOBÁRIC, and بقلة اللينه BUCK LÚT UL' LI-YE-NEH. Arabic names for Purslain.

(519) بقم BUCKUM. Redwood.

(520) بقيس BUCKUS. The box tree.

(521) بكبر BUCK-BIR. Caffia fiftularis.

p. *khyár chember.* خيارچنبر

(522) بكاين BUCKÁ-YIN. बकायन The Perfian lilac.

(523) پلاس پاپرا PÁLÁSSPÁPRÁ. पलासपापरा Seed of an Indian tree, called *péláh. vide* 528.

v. ढाककेबीज *dhák key beej.*

(524) بليلج BE-LEY-LUJ. Belleric myrobalans.

बहेरा h. *be-hey-rá.* p. *be-ley-leh.* بليله

qu. cold. *prop.* aftringent, attenuant, and tonic. *ch.* yellow, and ripe. *d.* one to three direms. *cor.* honey. *fuc.* emblic myrobalans.

(525) بلح BÉ-LUJ. Unripe dates.

कचीखजूर غوره خرما

h. *kutchee kehjoor.* p. *ghowreh khurmá.*

qu. cold and dry.

(526) بلادر BÉ-LÁ-DUR. Anacardium. भिलावा h. *beh-lá-wá.*

qu. hot and dry 4. *prop.* cephalic. *ch.* black, thick, and full of juice. *d.* one and a half direms. *cor.* fefami oil.

(527) بلس BÚ-LÚS. White fig.

p. *injeer fefeid.* انجير سفيد

(528)

(528) پلاس PELASS. पलास An Indian tree. ढाक h. v. *dhák.* p. *peleh* پله

(529) بلوط BELOOT. Acorn.

qu. cold and dry. *prop.* aſtringent, and ſtyptic.

(530) بلوطالارض BELOOT UL URZ. Gemander. p. *kemá-dry-oon.* كمادريوس

(531) بلوطالملك BELOOT UL MELIC. The Oak.

p. *ſháh beloot.* شاهبلوط

(532) پلنکمشك BE-LUNG-MISHK. A ſpecies of ſweet baſil.

(533) بلبوس BUL-BOOS. A ſpecies of wild onion.

(534) بيل BAYL. बिल An Indian fruit.

qu. hot and dry. *p.* aſtringent. *ch.* ſweet.

(535) پلاسپيپل PELASSPILPIL. पलासपीपल An Indian tree.

(536) پلول PULWUL. पलवल An Indian pulſe.

(537) بلسن BULSUN. A ſpecies of vetch.

मसूर h. *muſoor.* p. *ud-us.* عدس

(538) بلسان BU-LÉ-SÁN. The balſam. Tree of Egypt.

qu. hot and dry. *prop.* of the balſam, attenuant, and deobſtruent. *d.* half a direm. *cor.* ſandel wood. *ſuc.* olive oil, and caſſia lignia.

(539) پنجنکشت PUNJUN-GOOSHT. The agnus caſtus tree.

सँभालु h. *ſumbháloo.*

(540) بنفسج BEHUSSEJ. Violet.

बनफ़्सा h. *benoſá.* p. *benufsheh.* بنفشه

(541) بنج BUNJ. Black henbane ſeed.

(542) بندق BUNDOOK. Filbert.

v. *findook.* فندق

(543) پنجهمريم PUNJEH MIRIEM. Sowbread. हाथाजूरी h. *hát,há jooree.*

(544) بنطافلون PENTAFELOON. Cinquefoil.

(545) بن BUN. Coffee.

p. *tokhem keweh.* تخمقهوه

(546) بنسلوچن BUNS-LOW-CHUN. बंसलूचन Sugar of bamboo.

p. *tub-ſheer.* طباشير

(547) بن كيهون BUN-GEY-HOON. बनगेहें Wild wheat.

(548) پندالو PIND-A-LOO. पिंडालो An Indian eſculent root.

(549) بنتومه BUN-TOO-MEH. A ſpecies of dodder. आकासबेल h. *akáſs beyl.*

(550) پنبهدانه PUMBEH DA-NEH. Cot-

Cotton ſeed. बिनुला h. *bé-now-lá.*

(551) بندق هندي BUNDOOK HINDEE. An Indian nut.

रीठा h. *reet,hà.*

qu. hot and dry. *d.* twenty miſkals of the oil.

(552) بنج دشتي BUNJ DESHTEE. The thorn apple.

v. *jowz maſſil.* جوزماثل

(553) بوصير BOW SEER. Mullein.

(554) بورق BOORUC. Borax.

सुहागा تنكار بوره

h. *ſow-há-gá.* p. *tinkár.* v. *booreh.*

qu. hot and dry. *prop.* detergent, cauſtic, and emetic. *ch.* white, from Armenia. *d.* in clyſters, from one to two direms. *cor.* gum arabic. *ſuc.* bitter ſalt.

(555) بوم BOOM. *p.* The owl.

उलू h. *u-loo.*

(556) بوزيدان BOO-ZY-DÁN. A thick, white root, about four inches long.

qu. hot and dry. *prop.* attenuant. *ch.* thick, white, and ſtriped. *d.* one to two direms. *cor.* honey.

(557) بوقلمون BOO-KE-LEE-MOON. The chameleon. *vide* 136.

(558) پوپو POOPOO. *p.* The lapwing. a. *bud-hud.* هدهد

(559) پودنه POWDENEH. Garden mint.

(560) بورهارمني BOOREH URMENY. Borax. *vide* 554.

(561) بول BOWL. Urine. *ſháſheb* شاشه

(562) پوش دربندي POSH DERBENDEE. A plant growing in Derbend, which the natives bruiſe, and form into little bougies, and uſe as an eye-ſalve.

(563) پوي POW-EY. पुय A plant, which has tendrils like the vine, and bears a fruit reſembling fox's grapes.

(564) بولسري BOWL-SIR-EE. बोलसरी An Indian tree, whoſe fruit is a remedy for the toothach.

The flower has a pungency, which is increaſed by being dried.

(565) بهيرا BE-HEY-RÁ. बहेरा Belleric myrobalan.

(566) پهلسا PHULSÁ. फालसा An Indian fruit.

(567) بهرامج BEH-RÁ-MUJ. A ſpecies of willow.

p. *beid muſhk.* بيدمشك

(568) بهارامرود BEHAR UMROOD.

Pear-

Pear bloſſoms. p. *gool umrood.* گل امرود
prop. cephalic.

(569) بهوجپتر BHOWJ-PUTTER. भोजपत्र The bark of a tree, which is uſed in Caſhmeer for writing, inſtead of paper.

(570) بهانگ BHANG. भांग A ſpecies of hemp.

The leaves are narcotic and aphrodiſiac.

(571) بهرمان and بهرام BEHRAM, and BEHR-MÁN. *p.* Seed of baſtard ſaffron.

(572) پهکرمول PHO-KIR-MOOL. An Indian root. फोकरमुल

(573) بهمن BEH-MUN. A Perſian root.

It is ſomewhat like a carrot, but is hard, crooked, rough, and pungent. There are two ſpecies, white, and red. Both are deobſtruent and alſo accounted reſtorative.

(574) بهاربه BEHÁR BEH. Quince bloſſoms. p. *gool áb-ee.* گل آبي
prop. chephalic.

(575) پهتكري PHIT-KERRY. फिटकरी Alum. p. *ſhub yemenee.*

(576) بينت BEYNT. बिंत Rattan. p. *kayz-rán.* خيزران

(577. بيرزد BEER-ZUD. Galbanum. बेरजा h. *bir-ee-já.*

(578) بيدانجير BEID INJEER. The palma chriſti. *vide* 84.

(579) پيار PEE-YAR पेयार An Indian acid fruit, the ſeed of which is called *chorowngee.*

(580) بير BEIR. बिर A ſpecies of plum. p. *konar.* كنار
qu. cold and dry.

(581) پيپلامور PEEPLÁMOOL. पीपलामुल Root of the long pepper buſh.

(582) بيخ سوس BEYKH SOOS. Liquorice root. *vide* 180.

(583) بيش BEESH. A poiſonous root, brought from China.

(584) بيض BYZ. Egg in general. p. *tokh em jánwár.* تخم جانور h. *undá.* अंडा

(585) پيپل PEEPUL. पीपल Long pepper.

It is alſo one of the names of the banyan tree.

(586) بيل BAIL. बिल An Indian fruit, containing in a hard ſhell a pulp ſomewhat reſembling the apricot in flavour.
qu. dry 3.

(587) پيتل PEETUL. पीतल Braſs. p. *berunj.* برنج

(588) پيلو PEELOO. पीलु The toothpick tree. *vide* 90.

(589) پينو PEENOO. Dried milk curds. v. *keroot.* قروت

(590) بيخ شانه دشتي BEHK SHÁNEH DESHTEE. Root of the comb tree.
कंगनीकेजर h. *kunghnee key jir.*

(591) بيخ چوچي BEYKH CHOO-CHEE. The leech root.
चुचीकेजर h. *choochee key jir*, and जोंककीजर *jownk key jir.*
It is ſo called, becauſe the fruit of this plant ſticks like a leech.

ت

(592) تانبا TÁMBÁ तांबा Copper. p. *miſs.* مس

(593) تامر TÁ-MIR. The flower of ſorrel.
चुकेकेफुल گل حماض
h. *chooká key phool.* p. *gool hum-dz.*

(594) تانبول TÁM-BOOL. Betel leaf.
पान & नागबेल برگ تنبول
h. *pán*, and *nág-beyl.* p. *birg tumbowl.*

(595) تباشير TEBÁ-SHEER. Sugar of Bamboo. *vide* 546.

(596) تبر TIBR. Gold.
सोना h. *ſowná.* p. *zir*, زر and *tillá.* طلا

(597) تبكان TIB-KÁN. Any thorn.
कांटा *h. kán-tá.* p. *khár.* خار

(598) تبن مكه TIBN MUCKEH. Camel's hay. *vide* 63.

(599) تتريك TIT-REEK. ततरीक Sumach.

(600) تتلي TUTLEE. तेतली The leech plant. *vide* 592.

(601) تخ TUKH. Seſamé. Seed, after the oil has been expreſſed.
खल h. *khul.* p. *gun-já-reh.* كنجاره

(602) تخم TOKHEM. *p.* Seed, in general. बीज h. *beej.* *a.* *buzir.* بزر

(603) تذرج TE-ZURJ. Pheaſant. p. *teedero.* تدرو

(604) ترپهلا TRI-PHÉ-LÁ. त्रेफला General name for three kinds of myro-

ba-

balans. *vide* 204.

(605) ترابصيدا TIR-ÁB-SYDÁ. Sidonian earth.

(606) ترمرا TRI-MEE-RA. त्रिमरा A purgative feed.

(607) ترب TOORB. *p.* Radish. मुली h. *moolee.*

(608) تربد TURBID. Turbith root. निसवत h. *nis-wut,* and नागपतर *nágputter.*

prop. purgative. *ch.* China.

(609) ترمس TUR-MISS. Egyptian lupin.

(610) ترابالهالك TU-RÁB-UL-HÁLICK. Arsenic. संबोलखार h. *sumbool-khár.* a. *sum-ul-fár.* سم الفار

(611) ترنجبين TUREN-JEE-BEEN. A species of manna, collected at Khoresan. from a thorny plant, called *khár shooter.*

prop. mild purgative. *ch.* resembling manna, and which is brought from Nishápoor. *d* from seven to thirty direms. *cor.* tamarinds.

(612) ترياق روستايان TERIAC ROWSTYÁN. Garlic.

(613) ترياق الحيته TERIAC UL HIHYEH. A bezoer stone, which is found in the corner of the eye of a mountain ox.

(614) ترياق TERIÁC. Treacle. Antidotes of every kind against poisons. p. *pád-zeher.* پادزهر

(615) ترياق تركي TERIÁC TOORKEE. Mummy. v. *moo-mee-yi.* موميائي

(616) ترهتي TREHUTEE. त्रेहुती White kut,h.

कतसफेद v. *kat,h sefeid.*

(617) ترابالقي TU-RÁB-UL-KIE. The emetic earth, arsenick. *vide* 613.

(618) تشميزج TUSH MEEZUJ. A black shining seed, resembling that of quince. चाकसु h. *cháksoo.* p *cheshmuck.* چشمک

qu. hot and dry.

(619) تفاح TUFFÁH. Apple. p *seeb.* سيب

(620) تفاح الارض TUFFÁH UL URZ. Camomile flowers. v. *bá-booneh.* بابونه *vide* 363.

(621) تفاح الجن TUFFÁH UL GIN. Fruit of the mandrake.

(622)

(622) تفاح بري TUFFÁH BIR-REE. Medlar. v. *zá-roor.* زعرور

(623) تفاح ارمني TUFFÃH URMENEE. Apricot. v. *khoobánee.* خوباني

(624) تفاح پارسي TUFFAH PARSEE. Peach. v. *shuft-á-loo.* شفتالو

(625) تگرگ TÉ-GURG. Hailstone. उोला h. *owlá.* p. *jháleh.* ژاله

(626) تل TIL. तिल Sesamé seed.

(627) تلسي TULSEE. तोलसी Sweet basil.

p. *bádrunj boo yáh.* بادرنجبويه

(628) تلي TILLEE. तेली The milt, or spleen. p. *se-poorz.* سپرز

(629) تمساح TIM-SAH. Aligator. मगरमछ h. *mugur-mutch.* p. *nehung;* نهنگ

(630) تمر TEMR. Date.

खजुर h. *kehjoor.* p. *khurmá.* خرما

qu. hot and moist. *prop.* detergent, and restorative. *suc.* raisins.

(631) تمتم TUMTUM. Sumach.

v. *súmác.* سماق

(632) تمرهندي TEMR HINDEE. Tamarind. *vide* 325.

(633) تنكار TINCAR. Tincal. h. *so-bá gá.* सुहागा

(634) تن TUN. तेन A flower, used for dying yellow.

(635) توبال الحديد TÚBÁL UL HEDEED. Dross of iron. p. *cherk áhun.* چرک آهن h. *lo-háy ká-keet.* लोहेकेकीट

(636) توتياي زرد TOO-TEE-A ZIRD. The *Basrah* stone.

p. *sung busree.* سنک بصري

qu. cold 1, dry 2. *prop.* drying ulcers.

(637) تون TOON. तुन Flowers of the agnus castus tree.

(638) توت TOOT. Mulberry.

(639) توت وحشي TOOT WUSHEE. Blackberry. v. *áleek.* عليق and *toot seh gool.* توت سه كل

(640) تودري TOWDREE. Seed of mallows.

prop. deobstruent, and detergent. *eh.* yellow. *d.* half a miskal.

(641) توريي TU-RI-EY. तोरई An Indian pot-herb.

(642) تونبري TOOMBREE. तोंबरी. Two species of gourd, one sweet, and the other bitter.

S (643)

(643) تين TEEN. Fig. p. *injeer*, انجير *prop.* detergent, and ſuppurative.

(644) تيندو TEINDOO. तिं Fruit of the ebony tree.

ث

(645) ثافسيا SÁ-FEE SÁ. *g.* Gum of wild rue.

prop. cauſtic.

(646) ثالسقيس SÁ-LIS-KEES. Babylonian creſſes.

v. *berf babilee.* حرف بابلي

(647) ثدي SUD-EE. The dugs of any animal. p. *piſtan.* پستان

h. चुची *choochee*, and जुजीया *ju-jeeyá.*

(648) ثعلب SÁLEB. Fox.

h. लोंबरी *look bree*, and लमरी *loombree.* p. *ro-báh.* روباه

(649) ثعام SÁ-AM. White worm-ſeed.

p. *dirmeneh ſefeid.*

(650) ثغارير SÁGHÁREER. A ſmall ſpecies of melon, very delicious.

h. कचरी *kutch-e-ree.* p. *duſt-um-booyeh.* دستنبويه

(651) ثلج SULJ. Snow.

पाला h. *pá-lá.* p. *burf.* برف

(652) ثلج چيني SULJ CHEENEE. China ſnow, a ſoft white ſtone, uſed as a collyrium.

qu. cold and dry. *prop.* detergent. *d.* 2 dangs. *ſuc.* crab's eyes.

(653) ثوم SOOM. Garlic.

लःसुन h. *lehſun.* p. *ſeer.* سير

qu. hot and dry, 4. *prop.* attenuant. *ch.* large cloves. *d.* 3 cloves. *cor.* acids, oils, and greaſy food.

(654) ثيل SEEL. A ſpecies of thiſtle. *vide* 213.

ج چ

(655) چاب CHAP. चाब An Indian fruit tree.

(656) جاوشير JÁ-WE-SHEER. Gum opopanax. p. *gáwſheer.* گاوشير

qu. hot and dry, 2. *prop.* deobſtruent, attenuant, diaphoretic, and diſcutient. *ch.* of a ſaffron colour, eaſily diſſolving in water. When freſh

fresh taken from the tree it is white, but afterwards changes to yellow; the solution resembles milk. *d.* half a direm. *suc.* of sagapenum, twice the quantity.

(657) جارالنهر JÁR-UL-NEHR. A water plant. v. *seluck ul má.* سلق الماء

It resembles the *nelufir*, and appears just above the surface of the water.

(658) جاورس JÁ-WÉRS. A species of millet.

qu. cold and dry. *prop.* astringent. *cor.* oil of sweet almonds.

(659) جاسوس JÁSUS. A species of white poppy. p. *khush-kásh zub-e-dee.* خشخاش زبدي

(660) جايپهل JÁ-I-PHUL जायफल Nutmeg. p. *jowz bew-á.* جوزبوا

(661) جامن JAMUM, जामुन and پهلندا PHÉLINDÁ. फलनदा Names of an Indian fruit, resembling black grapes; it has a large stone.

qu. dry. *prop.* astringent.

(662) چاكسو CHÁK-SU. चाकसु A black seed, resembling that of quince.

(663) جامسه JA-ME-SEH. A species of lupin.

(664) جالي JÁ-LEE. The tooth-prick tree. पीलु h. *peeloo.*

(665) جبن JUBN. Cheese. p. *puneer.* پنير

(666) چتچرا CHIT-CHE-RA. चितचरा The inverted thorn. p. *khár-wáz-gooneh.* خاروازكونه

(667) چچندا CHE-CHEEN-DÁ. चिचडा A long kind of cucumber.

(668) جدوار JUD-WÁR. Zedoary. *vide* 398.

qu. hot and dry, 3. *prop.* an antidote against poisons. *ch.* China, which after grinding in water, is of a violet colour. *d.* half a direm to half a miskal. *cor.* coriander seed. *suc.* of zecumbád, three times the quantity.

(669) جدي JUD-EE. A kid. हलवान h. *hulwán.* p. *buz-gháleh.* بزغاله

(670) جرجيرالماء JIR-JER-UL-MÁÁ. A species of parsley, growing in marshy places.

(671) جراسيا JE-RÁ-SY-Á. Cherry. p. *áloo-bá-loo.* آلوبالو

(672) چرايتا CHE-RÁY-TÁ. चरायता The wormseed plant. a. *kussub us zereereh.* قصب الزريره

(673) جرتوت JIRTOOT. The wild egg plant. *vide* 382.

(674) جريث JEREES. The eel.

(675)

(675) جراد JE-RÁD. Locuſt. टिडी h. *tiddee.* v. *mul-uck.* ملخ

qu. hot and dry, 2. *prop.* ſudorific.

(676) جرادالبحر JE-RÁD-UL-BEHR. The ſea locuſt; a ſhrimp. झींगा h. *jheengá.* p. *mul-uck de-ree-á-iy.* ملخ دريايي

(677) جرجير JIRJEER. The herb rocket.

(678) جرجر JIR-JIR. A ſpecies of bean. p. *ba-ké-lá.* باقلا

(679) چرونجي CHEROWNJEE. चरौनजी A ſmall grain, reſembling pepper. p. *nuckel khójeh.* نقل خواجه

(680) جزمازج JUZ-MÁ-ZUJ. Fruit of the tamriſk.

qu. hot and dry, 1.

(681) جزر JUZ-IR. Carrot. गाजर h. *gáj-ir.* p. *guz-ir.* گزر and *zirduck.* زردک

prop. deobſtruent. *d.* 2 direms. *ſuc.* turnips.

(682) جزربري JUZ-IR BIRREE, & JUZ-IR AKLEETEE. جزراقليتي Wild carrot. v. *ſhe-ká-kul.* شقاقل p. *zirduck deſhtee.* زردک دشتي

(683) جست JUST जसत A ſpecies of tin. p. *roub tootyá.* روح توتيا

(684) جسمي JUSSMEE. A thorny plant. गुखरू h. *go-khroo.* v. *khár kuſ-uck.* خارخسك

It bears a prickly fruit, of a triangular form.

(685) جعده JOA-DEH. A ſpecies of wormſeed.

(686) چغندر CHOGHUNDER. *p.* Beet root. a. *ſe-luck.* سلق

(687) جفت البلوط JIST-UL-BE-LOOT. The outſide ſkin of an acorn.

(688) جفري JEF-REE. The envelope of the bud of a female palm tree.

(689) جليد JE-LEED. Ice. पाला h. *pá-lá.* p. *berf.* برف

(690) جلد JILD. Skin, leather. चमरा h. *chumrá.* p. *poſt.* پوست

prop. healing, and ſtyptic. *ch.* the ſkin of a ſucking animal.

(691) جلنار JULNÁR. Flowers of the barren wild pomegranate tree.

qu. cold 1, dry 2. *prop.* aſtringent. *b.* Perſian or Egyptian. *d.* 1 to 2 direms. *cor.* tragacanth, with oil of almonds.

(692) جلجلان JUL-JE-LAN. Dried coriander ſeed.

p. *kiſh-*

p. *kishnee khush.* کشنیزخشک

(693) جلنسرین JUL-NUS-REEN. The rose of Jericho, or dogrose.

p. *wurd-cheenee.* وردچینی

(694) جلنجبین JU-LEN GE-BEEN. Conserve of roses, made with honey.

p. *goolkund ássulee.* گل قند عسلی

(695) چلغوزه CHILGHOZÁ. *p.* Pine kernels. चलगुजा. h. *chil-go-já.*

(696) چلپاسه CHIL-PÁ-SEH. A Lizard. चिपकली h. *chip-kul-ee.*

(697) جلجلان الحبشي JULJULÁN-UL-HUBSHEE. Black poppy.

(698) جمست JUMUST. A kind of blue gem, found near Medina.

prop. cures palpitation of the heart, and fainting.

(699) جمد JUMED. *a.* Ice. *vide* 691. पाला h. *pá-lá.* p. *yekh.* یخ

(700) جمار JUMÁR. The pith of a palm tree. p. *puneer khurmá.* پنیرخرما

(701) جمیز JUMEEZ. Adam's fig. *vide* 268. p. *injeer adam.* انجیرآدم

(702) جمل JUMEL. A camel. ऊंट h. *oonte* p. *shooter.* شتر

(703) جمسفرم JUM-US-FERIM. A species of sweet basil.

(704) جمان JUMÁN. A wood, the outside of which is black, and the inside of a pistachio green. v. *jeeldaroo.* جیلدارو

prop. it destroys worms in the intestines.

(705) جمعیره JUM-EEREH. An Indian shrub. भंगरा h. *bhungrá.*

(706) جمدچینی JUM-ED CHENEE. Native alkaline salt. *vide* 129.

(707) جنطیانا JIN-TYÁ-NÁ. Gentian. *vide* 372.

qu. hot and dry 3. *prop.* deobstruent, and diaphoretic. *ch.* Europe, of a reddish brown, and bitter taste. *d.* half a miskal. *cor.* spleenwort, or rhubarb.

(708) چنپا CHUMPÁ. चम्पा An Indian flower tree.

prop. the seed is inebriating.

(709) جندبیدستر JUNDBEYDUSTER. Castor.

p. *goond-bey-duster.* گندبیدستر

qu. hot and dry 3. *prop.* attenuant, and diaphoretic. *d.* one quarter of a direm to one direm. *suc.* sweet flag.

(710) چندن CHUNDUN. चंदन White sandel wood.

p. *sundul sefeid.* صندل سفید

(711) جوزبوا JOWZ BEWÁ Nutmeg. *vide* 660.

(712) جوزالطيب JOWZ UT TEIB.

The same as the above.

(713) جوزالمرج JOWZ UL MUR-UJ. Winter cherry.

v. *hub kak-nej.* حب كاكنج

(714) جواكهار JEWÁ-KHÁR. जवाखार Native alkaline salt.

v. *nut-roon.* نطرون

(715) جوز JOWZ. Walnut. *vide* 46.

(716) چوک CHOOK. चूक Sorrel.

p. *hum-áz.* حماض

(717) جوزماثل JOWZ MÁSSEL.

The thorn apple. धतूरा h. *dhé-toorá.*

p. *gooz gee-ab.* كوزكياه

qu. cold and dry 4. *prop.* narcotic. *d.* one carat. *cor.* cotton.

(718) جوزالسرو JOWZ UL SIROE.

Fruit of the cypress tree.

qu. hot and dry 3. *prop.* styptic. *d.* one direm to half a miskal. *cor.* honey. *suc.* pomegranate peels.

(719) جوانسا JEWN-WÁ-SÁ

जवासा A thorny plant, of which they make purdehs.

(720) جوزالكوثل JOWZ UL KOW SUL. The physic nut. मैनफल h. *myn-phul.* p. *jowz ul kie.* جوزالقي

prop. emetic. *d.* one to two direms, in paralytic complaints. *suc.* white hellebore.

(721) جوزالرت JOWZ-UL-RET.

A saponaceous nut. रीठा h. *reethá.*

(722) جوزهند JOWZ HIND. Cocoa-nut. नारयल h. *nár-yel,* and खोपरा *khoprá.* p. *nárjeel.* نارجيل

(723) چولائي CHEW-LIE. चुलाई

An Indian pot-herb.

(724) چهر CHE-HUR. छड़ Spikenard.

vide 726.

(725) جهاوء JHÁ-OU. झाउ Tamarisk tree. *vide* 36.

(726) چهتامانسي JEHTE-MÁN-SEE. जटामासी Spikenard.

a. *sembel ut teib.* سنبل الطيب

(727) چيتا CHEEN-TÁ. चीता

A red root, that is very acrid and caustic. p. *shee-te-ruj.* شيطرج

(728) جيپال JY-PÁL. जैपाल

A purgative seed.

a. *hub-us-sul-á-teen.* حب السلاطين

(729) جيلدارو JEEL-DÁ-ROO.

vide

(730) چيده CHEE-DEH. चीड़

The lesser pine. a. *senobir seghár.*

(731)

ح

(731) حاشا HÁSHÁ. Thyme.

(732) حاج HAJ. The thorny plant, from which is collected the ſpecies of manna, called *terunjebeen*. *vide* 611.

(733) حافر HÁFIR. Hoof of any animal. खुर h. *khur*. p. سم *ſoom*.

prep. drying. *ch*. of clean animals. *cor*. oils. *ſuc*. horn.

(734) حافظالنحل HAFIZ UL NEHUL. Euphorbium. *vide* 254.

(735) حب HUB. Berry, ſeed.

बीज h. *beej*. फल *p,hul*. p. *dáneh*. دانه and *tokhem*. تخم

(736) حبحنكلا HUB HUNKILÁ. A grain reſembling black pepper; but which withinſide is white and ſweet.

v. *hub ſumneh*. حبالسمنه

(737) حبةالسودا HUBBUT-UL-SOWDÁ. Black ſeed.

कलौंजी h. *kerownjee*. p. *ſy-á dá-neh*. سياهدانه

(738) حبةالخضرا HUBBUT-UL-KHUZRA. Fruit of theturpentine tree.

prep. diaphoretic, and provocative. *ch*. large, green, freſh.

(739) حبقالماء HUBEK-UL-MÁ. Water mint. p. *powdneh ábee*. پودنهآبي

(740) حبالزبيب HUB-UZ-ZUBEEB. Grape ſtone.

दाखकेबीज h. *dák,h-key-beej*.

p. *tokhem meveez*. تخم مويز

(741) حبالقلت HUB-UL-KILT. A ſpecies of vetch. p. *máſh bindee*.

कोलथी h. *kult,hee*.

(742) حبقالتمساح HUBUK UL' TIMSÁH. Water mint; *vide* 739.

(743) حباليهود HUB-UL-YEHOOD. Winter cherry. *káhnuj*. كاكنج

(744) حبالعرعر HUB-UL UR-ÚR. Juniper berries.

(745) حبالصنوبرصغار HUB SENOBIR SEGHAR. Fruit of the leſſer pine. जीनदःकेबीज h. *jundeh key beej*.

p. *tokhem káj* تخم كاج and *ná-zow*. نازو

(746) حبالعصفر HUB UL USFER. Seed of ſafflower.

(747)

(747) حب البقر HUBUCK-UL-BUCKIR. Camomile flowers. *vide* 235.

(748) حب الخروع HUB-UL-KHIRWÁ. Seed of the palma chrifti.

अरंडकेबीज h. *árundé key beej.*

p. *tokhem beid injeer.* تخم بيد انجير

prop. difcutient and emollient; and taken internally to carry off redundant humours, and for cleanfing the blood. *d.* five to ten feeds, peeled.

(749) حبق HUB-UCK. Mint.

p. *powdeneh.* پودنه

(750) حب الملوک HUB UL MULOOK. A purgative feed.

p. *máboodáneh.* ماهودانه

(751) حب النيل HUB-UL-NEIL. A purgative feed.

h. *tokhem kunkwá.* تخم کنکوا

(752) حب القلقل HUB-UL-KILKIL. Seed of wild pomegranate.

p. *tokhem ánár defhtee.* تخم انار دشتي

(753) حب الاثل HUB UL USSOL. Tamarifk berries. p. *guzmazuck* گزمازک

(754) حب السفرجل HUB US SUFIR JUL. Quince feed.

बिहीकेबीज h. *behee key beej.*

p. *beh-dá-neh.* بهدانه

qu. cold and moift. *ch.* of the four quince. *d.* two direms. *cor.* fugarcandy. *fuc.* mallows feed.

(755) حب السلاطين HUB-US-SULÁTEEN. A purgative feed.

जमालगोटा: h. *jemálgowtá.*

p. *doond.* دند

(756) حب البلسان HU-BUL BULSÁN. Carpobalfam.

p. *tokhem bulfán.* تخم بلسان

prop. attenuant, and cardiac; detergent. *d.* two direms.

(757) حب القطن HUB UL KOTEN. Cotton feed. बिनुला h. *beynowla.*

p. *pumbehdáneh.* پنبهدانه

(758) حب البان HUB-UL-BÁN. Ben nuts.

qu. hot and dry. *ch.* large, fragrant. *d.* two direms. *fuc.* caffia lignea.

(759) حبه HUBBEH. A red feed, ufed as a weight by jewellers.

रत्ती h. *rutty.* p. *foorkh.* سرخ

(760) حبق الراعي HUBBUCK-UR-RIEY. Mugwort. *vide* 73.

(761) حب سجستاني HUB SEJISTÁNEE. Cardamums.

(762) حب نبطي HUB-UCK NUBTEE.

Garden mint.

p. *powdeneh boſtánee.* پودنەبستاني

(763) حبق صعتري HUBUCK SUCKREE, and حبق كرماني HUBUCK KERMÁNEE. Two names for ſweet baſil.

(764) حبق خراساني HUBUCK KHORÁSÁNEE. Sorrel.

(765) حجر اليشب HEJR UL YESHEB. Jaſper.

p. *ſung yeſhem.* سنك يشم

(766) حجر لابهت HEJR-UL-BEHUT. The eagle ſtone. *vide* No. 242.

(767) حجر الافروج HEJR UL UFROOJ. Pumice ſtone.

(768) حجر اليهود HEJR UL YEHOOD. Jew's ſtone, reſembling an olive. p. *ſung jehoodán.* سنك جهودان

(769) حجر البلور HEJR BELORE. Chryſtal. p. *ſung belore.* سنك بلور

(770) حجر البقر HEJR-UL-BUCKIR. A ſtone found in the gall bladder of an ox. p. *gáwzereh.* كاوزهره

(771) حجر النسر HEJR UL NESR. The eagle ſtone. *vide* 242.

(772) حجر الدم HEJR UL DUM. Bloodſtone. v. *ſhádenej.* شادنج

(773) حجر القمر HEJR UL KUMR. The moon ſtone; *vide* 493.

चंदरकांत h. *chánderkánt.*

(774) حجر المقناطيس HEJR UL MICKNATEES. The loadſtone.

चोमुकपाथर h. *chumuck put,hur.*

p. *ſung ahun-no-bá.* سنك آهن ربا

qu. hot and dry. *ch.* of a dark red, and that attracts iron ſtrongly. *d.* half a miſkal to one direm.

(775) حجر الكرك HEJR UL KIRK. A white ſtone, found on the banks of the Indus.

(776) حجر الرخام HEJR UL RÚKÁM. White marble.

(777) حجر الزيتون HEJR UL ZIETOON. The olive ſtone; another name for the Jew's ſtone. *vide* 768.

(778) حجر مشويه HEJR MESHEWYEH. Lime. चूनाकली h. *choonákullee.* p. *nooreh.* نوره

(779) حجر قبطي HEJR KIBTEE. The Coptic ſtone; a kind of fuller's earth.

(780)

(780) حجرارمني HEJR URMENEE. Bole armenee.

v. *gil urmenee.* كل ارمني

prop. purgative. *d.* half a direm to one miskal. *cor.* washing it.

(781) حجربحري HEJR BEH-REE. Coral. *vide* 417.

(782) حدج HUD-UJ. Dried coloquintida. p. *bunzil khooshk.* حنظل خشك

(783) حديد HE-DEED. Iron.

लोहा h. *lowhá.* p. *á-hun.* آهن

(784) حراشارومي HIR-Á-SHÁ ROOMEE. Wild mustard.

जंगली राई h. *junglee rie.*

p. *khirdul bir-ee.* خردل رومي

(785) حرف الماء HERF-UL-MÁÁ. A kind of water cresses.

(786) حرشف HIR-SHUF. Artichoke. v. *kungir.* كنكر

(787) حرف HERF. Seed of garden cresses.

p. *tokhem turreh teyzuck.* تخم تره تيزك

(788) حرمل HERMUL. Seed of wild rue. *vide* 114.

(789) حرجل HIRJUL. A species of locust without wings.

(790) حسك HUS-UCK. A small creeping plant.

qu. cold and dry, 1. *prop.* detergent, and deobstruent. *d.* two direms. *suc.* shepherd's staff.

(791) حشيش بزرالقطونا HESHEESH BUZIR-UL-KE-TOO-NÁ. Leaves of fleawort. p. *birg bungoo.* برک بنکو

qu. cold and moist.

(792) حشيش الزجاج HESHEESH-UZ-ZU-JÁJ. A water plant.

p. *gee-ah áb-geenáh.* کياه ابکينه

qu. cold and dry. *prop.* repellent. *d.* of the juice ten direms.

(793) حشيش الطحال HESHEESH UL TE-HÁL. Leaves of spleenwort.

vide 141. p. *jungee dároo.* زنکي دارو

(794) حشيش خراساني HESHESH KHORASANEE. Wormseed.

p. *dermeneh khorásánee.* درمنه خراساني

(795) حصرم HUSSRIM. Unripe grapes. कच्चीदाख h. *kutchee dákh.*

p. *ghowráh ungeer.* غوره انکور

prop. astringent. *cor.* aniseed and honey. *suc.* lemon juice.

(796) حضض HU-ZEEZ. Juice of lycium. रसवत h. *re-sowt.* p. *bu-lul.* هلل

prop. discutient, somewhat astringent, and styptic. *ch.* that of Mecca.

(797)

(797) حلبيب HULBEEB. A ſpecies of hermodactyls.

v. *ſoorenjan hindee.* سورنجان هندي

(798) حلتيت HILTEET. Aſafœtida. *vide* 305.

(799) حلزون HULZOON. Conch ſhell. संख h. *ſunkh.* p. *ſunj.* سنج

prop. drying.

(800) حلبه HULBEH. Fenugreek. मेथी h. *moohtee.* v. *ſhimlet.* شمليت

qu. hot and dry. *prop.* ſuppurative, and emollient. *d.* two direms; and in clyſters twenty direms. *cor.* oil of bitter gourd. *ſuc.* linſeed.

(801) حماما HO-MÁ-MA. Amomum. v. *mihlooj.* ماهلوج

prop. deobſtruent, and detergent. *ch.* Armenian, of a bright yellow, and fragrant. *d.* two direms.

(802) حماض الارنب HUMAZ UL URNEB. Dodder. v. *kuſhoos.* كشوث

(803) حماض الاترج HUMAZ-UL-UTREJ. Citron juice..

p. *turſheh turenj.* ترشه ترنج

qu. cold and dry.. *cor.* poppy juice.. *ſuc.* lemon juice.

(804) حماض البقر HUMAZ UL BUCKIR. Wood ſorrel. अमरूल

h. *ámrool.* p. *humáz birree.* حماض بري

(805) حماض نهري HUMÁZ NEHREE. Garden ſorrel. *vide* 813.

(806) حماض الامير HUMZ-UL-AMEER. A ſmall creeping plant.

(807) حمص HIM-IS. A kind of pulſe. चना h. *che-ná.* p. *nákhood.* نخود

(808) حمض HIMIZ. *a.* Glaſſwort. *vide* 163.

(809 حمر الارض HUMR-UL' URZ. Earth-worm. p. *kheráteen.* خراطين

(810) حمل HEML. A ram. बकरा h. *buckrá.* p. *bir eh* بره

(811) حمام HU-MAM. A pigeon. परेवा h. *purewá.* p. *kebooter.* كبوتر

(812) حماض بستاني HUMÁZ BOSTANEE. Garden ſorrel. *vide* 806. चूका h. *chooká.* p. *toorſheenuck.* ترشينك.

(813) حمار اهلي HY-MĀR AHLEE. The common aſs.

गदहा h. *gud-há.* p. *khur.* خر

(814) حمار وحشي HYMAR WEHSHEE. The onager, or wild aſs.

p. *gowr khur.* كورخر

(815) حنا HINNÁ. The ſhrub cyprus, uſed in dying. मिरहदी h. *mirh-dee.*

prop.

prop. aſtringent. *d.* for the cholic half a miſkal of the leaves; and as a cephalic two miſkals of the ſeed. *cor.* liquorice and tragacanth.

(816) حناي قريش HINNÁ-EY KOREISH. Moſs that grows on ſtones. v *buzáz us' ſuckher.* حزاز الصخر

(817) حنظل HUNZIL. Coloquintida. *vide* 306. p. *khirboozá telkh.* خربزه تلخ

qu. hot 3, dry 2. *prop.* purgative, and deobſtruent. *ch.* freſh, yellow, ripe. *d.* of the fruit from a carat to a direm; of the ſeed half a direm; or of the juice one dang and a half. *cor.* tragacanth, or maſtich. *ſuc.* wild rue.

(818) حنطه HINTEH. Wheat. गेहें h. *gee-hoon.* p. *gundum.* كندم

(819) حندقوقي HUNDKOKEE. *a.* The ſhrub lotus.

prop. attenuant, and diaphoretic. *d.* two direms. *cor.* endive.

(820) حوت HOOT. *a.* Fiſh. मछली h. *mutchlee.* v. a. *ſum-uck.* سمك p. *máhee.* ماهي

(821) حواري HE-WA-REE. Wheat flower. मैदा h. *mydá.* p. *arud gundum.* ارد كندم

(822) حي العالم HY-UL-ÁLUM. Houſeleek.

(823) حيه HI-YEH. A ſnake. सांप h. *ſámp,* and नाग *nág.* p. *már.* مار

خ

(824) خامالانق الذيب KHÁ-MÁ-LA-UNECK'UZ-ZEEB. Wolf's bane.

(825) خانق الكلب KHÁNECK UL KELB. Dog's bane, a poiſonous plant. कुचला h. *koo-che-lá.* p. *feloos máhee.* فلوس ماهي

(826) خارپشت KHÁR-POOSHT. The porcupine. साही h. *ſy-hee.* v. *kunfuz.* قنفذ

(827) خانق النمر KHÁNEK 'UN' NEMR. A poiſonous plant: a ſpecies of mezereon.

(828) خانق الملك KHÁNECK-UL-ME-LIC. Gall apple. p. *ſá-dá-we-rán.* سادوران

(829) خاماءاقطي KHÁ-MÁ-ÁKTEE. Danewort.

(830) خبث الحديد KOOBS-UL-HE-DEED. Droſs of iron.

लोहेकेकीट h. *lowhá key keet.* p. *reem ábun.* ريم آهن

(831) خبز KHUBZ. Bread. *vide* 27.

(832) خبث النحاس KHOOBS-UL-NOHASS. Dross of copper.

ताँबेकेकीट h. *támbáh key keet.*

p. *reem miss.* ريم مس

qu. hot and dry 3. *prop.* astringent, drying, caustic.

(833) خبث الرصاص KHOOBS UL RESÁSS. Dross of tin.

p. *reem kullie.* ريم قلعي

qu. cold and dry.

(834) خبث الفضه KHOOBS-UL-FIZEH. Dross of silver.

p. *cherk nokerá.* چرک نقره

(835) خبازي KHEBBAZEE. *a.* Mallows. *vide* 865.

(836) خرما KHURMÁ. Dates. *vide* 630.

(837) خربق اسود KHIRBUC USWUD. Black hellebore.

कुतकी h. *kootkee.*

qu. hot and dry 3. *prop.* purgative. *d.* half a direm. *cor.* oil of almonds, or tragacanth.

(838) خربق ابيض KHIRBUC ABIYUZ. White hellebore.

p. *khirbuc sefeid.* خربق سفيد

qu. hot and dry 3. *prop.* emetic. *ch.* white, brittle, and pungent. *d.* half a direm. *cor.* mastich. *suc.* nux vomica.

(839) خربوزه KHIRBOOZ. A grass, used for dying yellow. p. *supruc.* سبرک

(840) خروع KHIRWA. The palma christi plant. *vide* 84.

(841) خرنع KHIRFÁ. Fruit of the Ág tree. *vide* 248.

आगकाफल h. *ág-ká-phul.*

(842) خرفق KHIRFUC. Seed of wild rue. *vide* 114.

(843) خرچنك KHIRCHUNG. *p.* Sea crab. केकरा h. *keynkerá.*

p. *punj páiyeh.* پنج پايه

(844) خردل KHIRDUL. Mustard. राई h. *riey.*

prop. heating, promoting digestion, deobstruent.

(845) خراطين KHERÁ-TEEN. Earthworm. *vide* 276.

केचुवा h. *keynchewd.*

prop. promoting the growth of flesh in a wound.

(846) خراهين KHERU-HEEN. A leech. जोंक h. *joownk.* p. *zeloo.* ذلو

(847) خرفه KHURFA. Purslain. *vide* 433.

लो.

लोनिया h. *loonyá.*

(848) خرزهره KHIR-ZEREH. Rhododaphne.

(849) خرنوب شامي KHIRNOOB SHÁMEE. A species of bean. Carobs.

qu. cold and dry. *prop* astringent. *d.* five to ten direms. *suc.* acorns.

(850) خرنوب نبطي KHIRNOOB NUBTEE. Carobs.

qu. cold and dry. *prop.* astringent. *d.* 3 direms.

(851) خرنوب مصري KHIRNOOB MISREE. The fruit of the acorus thorn.

(852) خرنوب هندي KHIRNOOB HINDEE. Cassia fistularis. *vide* 521.

(853) خردل فارسي KHIRDUL FARSEE. Seed of wild rue. *vide* 114.

(854) خس KHUSS. Lettuce.

p. *káhoo.* كاهو

qu. cold and moist. *prop.* narcotic. *d.* two miskals. *cor.* parsley. *suc.* endive.

(855) خسرودارو KHUSROO-DAROO. Ganagal. *vide* 878.

(856) خسكدانه KHUSUC-DANEH. Seed of safflower.

(857) خشكار KHOOSHKÁR. Unsifted wheat flower. आटा h. *á-tá.*

(858) خشب الشونيز KHUSHUB-USH-SHOONEEZ. The black seed plant.

(859) خشخاش KHUSHKÁSH. Poppy. पोस्त h. *post.* p. *kooknár.* كوكنار

(860) خصية الثعلب KHUSYET-US'-SÁLEB. Satyrion.

qu. hot, and moist. *prop.* provocative. *d.* one to two miskals. *cor.* myrobalans.

(861) خصية الكلب KHUSYET-UL-KELB. A root resembling satyrion.

(862) خصية البحر KHUSYET-UL-BEHR. Castor. *vide* 164.

(863) خصيه KHUSYEH. Testicle.

पेलर h. *peyblir.* p. *khá-yeh.* خايه

(864) خضلاف KHUZLÁF. The Bdellium tree.

p. *derukht mokul.* درخت مقل

(865) خطمي KHITMEE. Marsh mallows.

prop. emollient, and suppurative. *ch.* that which bears a white flower. *suc.* mallows.

(866) خفاش KHE-FÁSH. A bat.

चमगीदर h. *chumgeedir.* p. *shub-purrek.* شبرك

(867) خلد KHULID. A muſk rat.

चकचुनदरी h. *chuck-choondree.*

p. *mooſh khoor.* موش کور

(868) خلاق KHE-LAK. The willow.

p. *derukht beid.* درخت بيد

qu. cold and dry. *prop.* drying *ch.* growing near a ſpring of water. *d.* of the juice twenty miſkals.

(869) خل KHULL. Vinegar.

p. *ſeerkeh.* سرکه

prop. attenuant. *cor.* ſugar, and oil of almonds.

(870) خلال KHELÁL. Unripe dates.

(871) خمر KHUMR. Grape wine.

दाखकामद h. *dákh ká mudh.* p. *ſheráb ungooree.* شراب انکوري

qu. hot and dry 3. *prop.* cordial. *d.* 72 miſkals.

(872) خمير KHUM-EER. Leaven.

p. *khum-eer má-yeh.* خميرمايه

(873) خمرالحمار KHUMR 'UL-HY-MÁR. A kind of ſoap aſhes.

साजी h. *ſájee.* p. *uſh-kár.* اشخار

(874) خمان KHÉ-MÁN. The elder tree.

(875) خنثي KHUNSÁ. Aſphodel.

qu. cold and dry. *prop.* detergent. *d.* five direms of the leaves; or of the buds and fruit two direms. *ſuc.* valerian.

(876) خوخ KHOWKH. Peach.

p. *ſhooſt-á-loo.* شفتالو

prop. correcting the bile.

(877) خوخ اقرع KHOWKH ÁK-RÁ. Indian leaf. v. *ſádij hindee* ساذج هندي

(878) خولنجان KHOW-LIN-JÁN. Galangal. कोलिंजन h. *koolinján.*

(879) خواجه کياه KHOW-JEH GEE-AH. An Indian ſhrub. बांसा h. *bán-ſá.*

(880) خيارشنبر KHY-A'R SHEM-BIR, and خيارچنبر KHY-A'R CHUMBIR. Caſſia fiſtularis.

अमलतास h. *amul-táſs.*

prop. purging bile. *ch.* Indian, black, full of grains, perfectly ripe, and with a thin ſkin. *d.* five to fifteen direms. *cor.* oil of almonds, and aniſeed, with an infuſion of tamarinds. *ſuc.* manna, with raiſins, and turbith root.

(881) خيار KHY-AR. Cucumber.

खीरा h. *kee-rá.*

p. *bád-rung.* بادرنك

qu. cold and moiſt.

(882) خيزران KYZ-RÁN. Rattan.

p. *choob beynt.* چوب بينت

qu. hot and dry. *prop.* expelling gravel. *d.* two direms. *cor.* hempagrimony. *ſuc.* bramble root.

د

(883) دارفلفل DÁR FILFIL. Long pepper. *vide* 18.

(884) دارشيشعان DÁR-SHEE-SHÁN. An acromatic bark.
h. *ká-iy-p,hul.* कायफल

(885) داكه DÁK,H. दाख Grapes.
a. *in-ub.* عنب p. *ungoor.*

(886) دارچيني DÁR-CHEE-NEE. Cinnamon. दालचीनी h. *dál-cheenee.*

(887) دجاج DUJÁJ. The houfe hen.
ककरा h. *kuckree.* p. *má-keyán.* ماكيان

(888) دخن DOKHN. Millet.
चीना h. *cheyná.* p. *arzun.* ارزن

(889) دخان DUKHÁN. Smoke.
धुंवा h. *d,hoon-án.* p. *dood.* دود

(890) دردي الخمر DOORDEE UL KHUMR. Dregs of wine.
p. *doord fherâb.* دردشراب

(891) درخت كل چكان DERUKHT GOOLCHUCKAN. The *mehwá* tree.
महुवा h. *mehewá.*

(892 درمنه DIRMENEH. Worm-feed. *vide* 224.

(893) درونج عقربي DEROONUJ ÁK-RUBEE. A root, refembling the tail of a fcorpion. अतुस h. *átus.*

qu. hot and dry, 3. *prop.* attenuant, and cardiac. *d.* half to one direm. *cor.* anifeed. *fuc.* civet.

(894) دستنبويه DUSTUMBOO-YEH. *p.* A fmall fpecies of melon, very delicious. कचरी h. *cutchree.*
a. *fhe-mám.* شهام

(895) دفلي DIFLEE. Rhododaphne.
कनेर h. *ke-neir.*

qu. hot and dry, 3. *prop.* difcutient. *ch.* large leaves, very bitter. *d.* half a direm.

(896) دلب DOOLB. The plane tree.
p. *derukht chenár.* درخت چنار

prop. drying. *fuc.* pomegranate peel.

(897) دم DUM. Blood.
लहु h. *lohoo.* p. *khoon.* خون

(898) دماغ DE-MAGH. Brains.
बिहेजा h. *bhey-já.*
p. *mughzfir.* مغزسر

(899) دم الاخوين DUM UL AKH-WEIN. Dragon's blood.
बीर

हीराउकी h. *beerá-dowkee.*

p. *khoon sy-owshán.* خون سیاوشان

prop. astringent, and styptic. *d.* half a direm. *suc.* gum arabic.

(900) دم الثعبان DUM ÚS SO-BÁN. Another name for dragon's blood.

(901) دند DUND. A purgative seed. *vide* 387.

(902) دوسر DU-SIR. Wild wheat. *vide* 48.

(903) دود الحریر DOOD-UL-HER-EER. The silkworm. p. *ke-rem-ubreyshum.* کرم ابریشم also *ke-rem-peelah.* کرم پیله

(904) دود القرمز DOOD UL KEER-MUZ. The *kermes* insect.

(905) دوض DOOZ. *a.* Water in which a red hot iron has been slaked.

(906) دوغ DOOGH. *p.* Buttermilk. छाच h. *chhátch*, and मठा *mutha.*

(907) دوالك DEWÁLIK. A species of moss.

(908) دوم DOWM. The tree which yields bdellium.

p. *derukht mokul.* درخت مقل

qu. hot and dry. *prop.* suppurative and attenuant. *ch.* fresh, of a yellow colour. *d.* one direm. *cor.* mastich.

(909) دونه ترکی DOONEH TUR-KEE. A species of aniseed.

जुरीअजवाइं h. *jooree ajwein.*

(910) دهنیا DEHNYÁ. धनिया Coriander seed. p. *kishneez.* کشنیز

(911) دهن DUHN. Oil.

तेल h. *tail.* p. *roghen.* روغن

(912) دیک DEEK. The dunghill cock.

कुकर h. *ko-kir.* p. *kheroos.* خروس

(913) دیوک DEEWUCK. The white ant.

दीमक h. *deemuck.* a. *urzeh.* ارضه

(914) دیوچه DEWCHEH. *p.* The leech. जोंक h. *joownk.* p. *zéloo.* زالو

ذ

(915) ذباب ZUBAB. The common fly. मक्खी h. *muck-bee.* p. *mug-us.* مگس

qu. hot and dry. *p.* emollient and emetic.

(916) ذبل ZU-BUL. Tortoise-shell. p. *post sungpost.* سنگ‌پشت

(917) ذراریح *a.* ZE-RA-REEH. Cantharides.

prop. blistering. *cor.* new milk, and oil of almonds.

(918) ذلو ZE-LOO. The leech. *vide* 906.

(919) ذنب‌الغار ZENUB-UL FAR. Ribwort.

(920) ذهب ZEHUB. Gold. सोना h. *sowna.* p. *zir.* زر

prop. cardiac. *d.* one carat of gold leaf. *cor.* honey and musk.

(921) ذيب ZEEB. The wolf. भेड़िया h. *beruba.* p. *gurg* گرگ

ر

(922) رانا RA-NA. *a.* Pomegranate. डालिम h. *dá-rim.* p. *anár.* انار a. *ruman.* رمان

(923) رازيانج RA-ZEE-A-NEJ. A species of aniseed.

prop. deobstruent, and diaphoretic.

(924) راتينج‌رومي RA-TEE-NEJ ROOMEE. Turpentine of fir. p. *zung-bá-ree.* زنگباري

(925) راوند RAWEND. Rhubarb. रेवंचीनी h. *rey-wun cheenee.* p. *rey-wend* ريوند

(929) راس RASS. The head of any animal. मुन्ड h. *moond,* and *seer.* p. *sir.* سر

(927) رال RAL. Pitch. p. *keer.* قير

(928) راسن RA-SUN. Elecampane.

prop. attenuant. *d.* one miskal.

(929) رب‌السوس RUB-US-SOOS. Liquorice juice. v. *usáreh mehuc.* عصارهٔ‌مهک

(930) رشاد RE-SHAD. Garden cresses. हालिम h. *hálim.* p. *tur-eh teyzuc.* تره‌تيزک

(931)

(931) رصاص RE-SASS. Tin. *vide* 86.

(932) رطب RU-TUB. Dates.

p. *khurmá*. خرما

(933) رعي الحمام RA-IY UL HU-MÁM. Valerian.

(934) رقعه RUK-ÁH, Is the name of a red root; and in general it used to signify all medicines that are applied to fractured limbs.

(935) رکت پهپ RUCKUT PHUP. रकतफप The red-flowered Rhododaphne. लालकनेर h. *lálkeneer*.

p. *khirzereh soorkh*. خرزهره سرخ

(936) رماد RÉ-MÁD. Ashes. राख h. *rákh*. p. *khá-kister*. خاکستر

prop. drying. *ch.* the ashes of acorns. *d.* half a direm.

(937) رمان البر RUMÁN UL BIR. A tree resembling the pomegranate, but smaller. The seed is called *hub kilkel*. The root thereof is called *mughar*.

(938) رمان حامض RUMÁN HUMÁZ. The sour pomegranate.

p. *anár toorsh*. انارترش

qu. cold and dry. *d.* ten wuckyeh of the juice. *suc.* juice of unripe grapes.

(939) رند RUND. The laurel. *v.* *mowrid*. مورد

(940) رنف RUNF. An odoriferous plant. v. *beid mishk*. بیدمشک

(941) روپا RU-PÁ. रुपा Silver.

p. *nok-rá*. نقره

(942) روناس RU-NÁS. Madder.

मजीठ h. *mé-jeet,h*.

(943) روباه تربک RO-BÁ TUR-BUC. Nightshade.

v. *inub us sá-leb*. عنب الثعلب

(944) روي ROW-EY. A kind of brass. कांसा h. *kan-sá*. a. *soofr*. صفر

(945) رهشي REH-SHEE. Sesamé meal.

(946) ريباس REE-BASS. The rhubarb root, or rhapontic.

(947) ريش REESH. A feather. पंख: h. *punk,h*. p. *pur*. پر

(948) ريحان RI-HAN. Sweet basil.

कालीतोलसी h. *ká-lee tulsee*.

p. *naz-bu*. نازبو

(949) ريه REE-YEH. The lungs. फेफरा h. *p,hep,hrá*. p. *shush*. شش

(950)

ز

(950) زاج ZAJ. General name for all the kinds of vitriol.

(951) زبيب ZE-BEEB. Raisins. किशमिश h. *kishmish.* p. *me-weez.* مويز

prop. emollient, and suppurative. *d.* ten direms. *suc.* jujules.

(952) زبد ZUBD. Butter. मक्खन h. *muckhun.* p. *muskeh.* مسكه

(953) زباد ZUBÁD. Civet.

(954) زبدالبحر ZUBD'UL-BEHR. Foam of the sea. समंदर्फेन h. *semunder-pheen.* p. *kefdery-á.* كف دريا

prop. detergent. *ch.* yellow. *d.* one to two dangs. *suc.* bole armenic.

(955) زبل ZIBL. Dung. लीद h. *leed.* p. *sirgeen.* سركين

(956) زجاج ZUJAJ. Glass. *vide* 26.

(957) زدوار JUDWÁR. Zedoary. v. *judwár.* جدوار

(958) زراوندمدحرج ZERAWEND MUDEHRUJ. Round birthwort. p. *zerawund geerd.* زراوندكرد

prop. attenuant, and deobstruent. *ch.* thick, of a saffron colour. *d.* one miskal to two direms. *cor.* honey. *suc.* zerumbád.

(959) زراوندطويل ZERA-WEND TE-WEEL. Long birthwort. p. *zerawend dráz.* زراونددراز

prop. deobstruent, discutient, and healing. *ch.* of a saffron colour, and thicker than the thumb.

(960) زرنيخ سرخ ZER-NEEKH SOORKH. Red orpiment. *vide* 113.

(961) زرنباد ZÉRUMBAD. कचूर h. *kutchoor.*

prop. attenuant, cardiac, and tonic. *d.* one direm.

(962) زرنيخ زرد ZER-NEEKH ZIRD. Yellow orpiment. *vide* 101.

prop. corrosive; poisonous.

(963) زرسود ZIR-SOOD. Turmeric. हलदी h. *huldee.* p. *zird choobeh.* زردچوبه

(964) زرير ZIREER. Milelot. *vide* 138.

(965) زرشك ZERISHK, and ZE-RUNG. زرنك Barberries.

(966) زرتك ZIR-TUCK. Juice of safflower. रंगकुसंभ h. *rung-kesumbh.* p. *áb khusac.* آب خسق

(967) زعرور ZU-ROOR. The medlar. p. *ke-yul.* كيل

prop. astringent. *ch.* red, ripe.

(968) زعفران ZÁ-FRÁN. Saffron.

कि

केसर h. *key-ſir.*

prop. diſcutient, deobſtruent, ſuppurative, exhilirating, and narcotic. *d.* half to one direm. *cor.* aniſeed.

(969) زغال ZU-GHÁL. Charcoal. कोइला h. *kowylá.*

(970) زغن ZUGHUN. The kite. चील h. *cheel.* p. *guleewáz.* غليواز

(971) زفت ZIFT. Pitch.

prop. diſcutient and detergent. *ch.* clean and gloſſy. *ſuc.* opoponax.

(972) زقوم ZÉ-KOOM. A thorny tree. सिंहद h. *ſynhud,* and थोर *thew-er.*

(973) زمرد ZUM-U-RUD. Emerald. पना h. *punná.*

(974) زنجبيل رطب ZUNJEBEEL RUTB. Green ginger. *vide* 55.

(975) زنجار ZUNJÁR. Verdegris. p. *zungár.* زنكار

prop. detergent.

(976) زنجفر ZUNJEFIR. Cinnabar. ईंगुर *ingoor.* p. *ſhungerf.* شنكرف

prop. poiſonous. *cor.* ghee and warm water.

(977) زنكبار ZUNGBÁR. Blue vitriol. नीलाथोथा h. *nee-la tho-thá.*

(978) زنجرف ZUNJERF. Cinnabar. *vide*

(979) زنجبيل ZUNJEBEEL. Dry ginger. सोंठ h. *ſownth.*

(980) زنكارمعدني ZUNGAR MAADENEE. Green vitriol. p. *tootya ſubz.* توتياي سبز

(981) زنجبيل شامي ZUNJEBEEL SHÁMEE. Elecampane. v. *rá-ſun.* راسن

(982) زوفاء رطب ZU-FÁ-IY RUTB. A filthy ſubſtance found on the tails of the Armenian ſheep, ſaid to be owing to their feeding on a milky kind of graſs, that is very heating.

prop. ſuppurative, and emollient. *ch.* very greaſy. *cor.* roſes.

(983) زوفاي يابس ZU-FA-IY YE-Á-BUS. Hyſſop.

prop. attenuant, ſuppurative, diaphoretic, and deſtroying worms in the inteſtines. *ch.* that which is brought from Jeruſalem. *cor.* gum arabic. *ſuc.* mint and maiden hair.

(984) زيرا ZEE-RA. जीरा Cumin ſeed. a. *ki-moon.* كمون

(985) زيت ZI-ET. Olive oil.

ch. fresh. *cor.* honey.

(986) زيبق ZEE-BUC. Quickfilver. *vide* 15.

qu. hot and dry. *prop.* hurtful. *ch.* that which has never been ufed.

(987) زيتون ZIE-TOON. The olive tree and fruit. जलपाई h. *julpaïy.*

س

(988) ساج SÁJ. A foreft tree.

साल h. *fál.*

(989) سابر SA-BIR. साबर An Indian animal, whofe fkin is ufed for fword fcabbards.

(990) سادج هندي SÁDIJ HINDEE. Indian leaf.

तेजपात h. *teyj-pát.*

(991) سارس SÁ-RESS. An Indian bird, of the ftork kind. सारस

(992) سانبهر لون SÁMBHER-LOON. सांबरलोन Rock falt.

(993) ساكون SÁ-GOON. सागुन An Indian tree, whofe leaves are compared to elephant's ears.

(994) ساجي SÁ-JEE. साजी A kind of foap afhes.

(995) ساتهي SÁTHEE. साथी A fpecies of red rice.

(996) سبج SUB-EH. Jet.

p. *fheb-eh.* شبه

(997) سپستان SEEPISTÁN. Sebeftens. लसोरा h. *lehfcorá.* p. *fugpiftán.* سك پستان

prop. emollient and fuppurative. *ch.* full of pulp. *d.* 16 to 30. *cor.* myrobalans. *fuc.* jujubes.

(998) سپندان SE-PEN-DÁN. Wild rue. *vide* 114.

(999) سپاري SU-PÁ-REE. सुपारी Areca nut; betelnut. a. *fooful.* فوفل

(1000) سداب SUD-ÁB. Rue.

सातरी h. *fá-tu-ree.*

prop. difcutient, diaphoretic, and anthelmentic. *d.* three direms. *cor.* anifeed.

(1001) سدر SEYDIR. A fpecies of plum tree. बेरकारूख h. *beyr ká rookh.* p. *derukht konár.* درخت كنار

prop. aftringent. *ch.* broad leaves. *d.* three direms of the leaves. *cor.* tragacanth.

(1002) سرب SOORB. Lead.

सीसा *feefá.*

(1003)

(1003) سرنج SOO-RUNJ. Red lead. *vide* 120.

(1004) سرخس SIRUKHS. A black root.

prop. deobſtruent, and drying. *ch.* black, and large, with the inſide of a piſtachio green.

(1005) سرشف SIR SHUF. Muſtard. सरसुन h. *ſir-ſoon.*

(1006) سرمق SIR-MUC. Orach. *vide* 403.

(1007) سرو SIR-OE. The cypreſs tree.

(1008) سرطان SIRTAN. The crab. *vide*

ch. the water crab.

(1009) سركه هندي SIR-KEH HINDEE. Bread ſoaked in water, and kept in the ſun till it becomes ſour. *vide* 25.

(1010) سعد SOÁD. Root of an odoriferous graſs. मोथा h. *mowtha.*

prop. diaphoretic, cardiac and tonic. *ch.* that brought from Cufah. *d.* one direm. *ſuc.* cinnamon and ſweet flag.

(1011) سعتر SÁ-TUR. An odoriferous plant. सातर h. *ſather.*

(1012) سفرجل SUFIR-JUL. Quince. *vide* 28.

prop. aſtringent, ſtyptic, cardiac, and tonic. *d.* ten direms of the juice. *cor.* dates, or honey. *ſuc.* pears.

(1013) سقمونيا SUC-MOO-NYÁ. Scammony. महमुद h. *meh-moo-deh.*

prop. cathartic. *ch.* that brought from Antioch; clean and light, gloſſy, of the colour of raw-ſilk, and eaſily friable. *d.* a carat, to two dangs.

(1014) سكبينج SUG-BEE-NUJ. Gum ſagapenum.

prop. deobſtruent, attenuant, and expelling gravel and ſtone. *d.* one direm to one miſkal. *cor.* liquorice.

(1015) سكر SUKHIR. Sugar. चीनी h. *chenee.* p. *ſhuckir.* شكر

prop. detergent, and emollient. *d.* twenty direms.

(1016) سك انكور SUG UNGOOR. Dog's grapes; nigthſhade. a. *inub us ſaleb.* عنب الثعلب

(1017) سكنجبين SE-KUN-JE-BEEN. Oxymel of vinegar and honey.

prop. emetic.

(1018) سلق الماء SULK-UL-MAA. A water plant. *vide*

(1019) سلت SELT. A ſpecies of barley. p *jow birheneh.* جوبرهنه

(1020) سلاجت SA-LA-GET. A ſpecies of ſtorax.

(1021) سلارس SIL-ÁRRUS. Liquid ſtorax

ſtorax. v. *me-áy-ſá-ye-leb.* ميعهسايله

(1022) سلق SULK. Beet root.

p. *chogbundir.* چغندر

prop. diſcutient, attenuant, detergent. *ch.* white. *cor.* vinegar. *ſuc.* turneps.

(1023) سلم SUL-UM. The gum arabic tree. *vide* 400.

(1024) سلجمي SULJUM. Turnep.

p. *ſhul-ghum.* شلغم

prop. diaphoretic. *ſuc.* carrots.

(1025) سليخه SE-LEE-KHEH. Caſſia lignea. तज h. *tuj.*

(1026) سم SUM. Poiſon in general.

बिस h. *biſs.* p. *ze-her.* زهر

(1027) سم الحمار SUM-UL-HYMÁR. Rhododaphne.

(1028) سم الفار SUM-UL-FÁR. Rat's bane. Realgar.

p. *murgh mooſh.* مرگ موش

(1029) سمور SUN-OOR. The ſable, or marten. *vide* 332.

(1030) سمندر SEMUNDER. The ſalamander.

(1031) سماروغ SE-MA-ROUGH. Muſhroom.

(1032) سُماق SU-MÁK. Sumach.

prop. aſtringent, and cardiac. *ch.* freſh, and red. *cor.* maſtich. *ſuc.* lemon juice.

(1033) سَماق SÉ-MÁK. A ſmall grain. कंगनी h. *kungnee.*

(1034) سمك SE-MUC. Fiſh. मछली h. *mutchlee*, and मीन *meen.* p. *má-hee.* ماهي

(1035) سم السمك SUM-UL-SE-MUC. A poiſonous milky graſs, bearing a yellow flower.

p. *má-hee ze-ruj.* ماهي زيرج

(1036) سمسم SOM-SOM. Seſamé ſeed. तिल h. *til.* p. *kunjed.* كنجد

(1037) سمن SE-MUN. Ghee.

घी h. *ge-hew.* p. *roghen gáw.* روغن كاو

(1038) سُمن SU-MUN. The lily of the valley.

(1039) سمندرلون SEMUNDER-LOON. समदर्नोन Sea ſalt.

p. *nemuc de-ry-á.* نمك دريا

(1040) سنا SUN-Á. Senna.

p. cathartic. *ch.* that which grows about Mecca. *d.* 4 to 7 direms in infuſion, or in ſubſtance 3 direms. *cor.* yellow myrobalans, roſe leaves, gum arabic, and tragacanth.

(1041)

(1041) سنگهارا SIN,GHA,RÁ. सिंघारा A prickly fruit.

It is of a triangular form, about the ſize of a filbert, and is produced by a plant that grows on the ſurface of the water.

(1042) سنبل الطيب SEMBEL UT-TIEB. Indian ſpikenard.

(1043) سنجاب SON-JÁB. The grey ſquirrel.

(1044) سنور SE-NORE. The cat. बिल्ली h. *billee.* p. *goorbeh.* گربه

(1045) سندروس SUNDROOS. Sandarach.

prop. drying. *ch.* tranſparent. *d.* half a miſkal.

(1046) سن SUN. सन Hemp. a. *kennub.* قنب

(1047) سنكه SUNKH. संख Conch ſhell. p. *ſefeid mohreh.* سفيدمهره

(1048) سنبل هندي SEMBEL HIN-DEE. Indian ſpikenard. *vide* 1042.

(1049) سنبل رومي SEMBEL ROO-MEE. Celtic nard. v. *nárdeen.* ناردين

(1050) سوسپند SOOSPUND. A ſpecies of milky graſs. दोदिही h. *dood-hee.* p. *ſheer-geeáb.* شيرگياه

(1051) سوسمار SOOSMÁR. The guana. गुहसांप h. *go-eh ſámp,h.*

(1052) سويق SÁ-WECK. Any grain fried and then ground into flour. सातू h. *ſá-too.*

(1053) سورنجان SU-REN-JÁN, Hermodactyls. *vide* 179.

जंगलीसिंघारा h. *junglee ſing,há,rá.*

(1054) سوسن SO-SUN. The lily.

(1055) سونچرلون SOWNCHUR-LOON. सोंचलोन Salt of bitumen. p. *nim-uck ſee-áh.* نمک سياه

(1056) سورن SOORUN. सोरं An Indian root, called alſo BUJ-IR-KUND. बजरकंद

(1057) سونتهه SOWNT,H. सोंठ Dry ginger. p. *zunjebeel.* زنجبيل

(1058) سوري SOOREE. सोरी A ſpecies of red vitriol, uſed by ſhoemakers.

(1059) سهاگا SO-HA-GÁ. सुहागा Tincal. p. *tin-kár.* تنكار

(1060) سهورا SEHOWRÁ. सहोरा An Indian tree, which it is pretended no ſnake will approach.

(1061) سير SEER. Garlic. लहसुन h. *lehſun.*

(1062) سيكران SIEK-RÁN. Black henbane ſeed. a. *buzir-ul-bung.* بزرالبنج

(1063) سيندهالون SINDAHLOON. सेंधालोन Rock ſalt. p. *nimuck ſung.* نمك سنك

(1064) سيسون SEE-SOON. सिसुन An Indian foreſt tree.

(1065) سياهدانه SEE-AH DÁNEH. Black ſeed. कलौंजी h. *kelownjee.*

ش

(1066) شاهلوج SHAHLOOJ. A ſpecies of yellow plum. p. *ſháh áloo.* شاه آلو

(1067) شاهترج SHÁHTERUJ. Fumitory. पितपापरा h. *pit-páp-rá.* p. *ſháhtereh.* شاهتره

prop. deobſtruent, detergent, and cathartic. *ch.* green, bitter. *d.* of the juice half a rutel. *cor.* lemon juice and honey. *ſuc.* ½ the weight of ſenna.

(1068) شاماخ SHAMÁKH. A grain. सांवां h. *ſán-wá.*

(1069) شاهانجير SHÁHINJEER. A ſpecies of fig. p. *injeer vizeeree.* انجيروزيري

(1070) شاهبلوط SHÁH BELOOT. Acorns. v. *beloot ul melic.* بلوطالملك

prop. aſtringent. *cor.* ſugar, or honey. *d.* two direms.

(1071) شاهدانق SHÁHDÁNUC. The inebriating hemp ſeed. p. *tokhem bung.* تخم بنك

(1072) شادنج SHADENUJ. Blood-ſtone.

(1073) شالوك SHÁHLOOK. शालुक An Indian root.

(1074) شاهسفرم SHÁ-HUS-FÉ-RUM. Sweet baſil. v. *ri-hán.* ريحان

(1075) شاهبوي SHÁH-BOO. Ambergris. v. *umbir.* عنبر

(1076) شانهدشتى SHÁ-NEH DESHTY. The comb tree, *vide* 590. कंगही h. *kungh-nee.*

(1077) شب SHUBB. Alum. *vide* 575.

(1078) شبت SHIB-IT. Fennel. सोवा h. *ſow-á.*

prop. ſuppurative, and narcotic. *d.* two direms.

(1079) شبرم SHIB-REM. A ſpecies of ſpurge.

(1080)

(1080) شبيبي SHE-BI-BEE. A narcotic root. The inebriating hemp-feed alfo bears this n·me.

(1081) شجرةالدب SHEJERUT'UL-DUB. The bear's tree; the medlar tree.

(1082) شجرةالحيات SHEJERUT ULHY-ÁT. The tree of life; the cyprefs.

(1083) شجرةالبراغيث SHEJERUT UL BERAGHEES. Hemp agrimony.

(1084) شجرةالموسي SHEJERUT UL MOOSA. Mofes's bufh; the bramble.

(1085) شحم SHÉ-HUM. Greafe of any animal.

चरबी h. *chirbee*. p. *peeh*. پيه

(1086) شحمحنظل SHE-HUM HUNZEL. The pulp of the coloquintida fruit. p. *mughz hunzel*. مغزحنظل

prop. emollient.

(1087) شراب SHÉ-RÁB. *p.* Wine; alfo all kinds of fherbets.

(1088) ششتره SHESHTEREH. Valerian. v. *foob*. فوه

(1089) شعير SHE-EER. Barley. p. *jow*. جو

(1090) شعر SHÁIR. Hair. बाल h. *bál*. p. *moo*. موي

(1091) شقاقل SHE-KÁ-KUL. Wild carrot.

(1092) شقايقالنعمان SHE-KA-YEK-UL-NÁMÁN. The anemone. p. *gool lá-leh*. كللاله

(1093) شلجم SHULJUM. Turnep. p. *fhulghum*. شلغم

(1094) شمليت SHIM-LEET. Fenugreek. मेथी h. *meet,hee*.

(1095) شمشاد SHUMSHÁD. The box tree.

(1096) شمع SHUMÁ. Bees wax. p. *moom*. موم h. *mehdoomul*. मधुमल

(1097) شنبليد SHUMBELEED. Flower of the hermodactyl plant. p. *gool foorenján*. كلسورنجان

(1098) شونيز SHOONEEZ. Black-feed. p. *fee-áh dáneh*. سياهدانه

prop. detergent, deftroying worms, difcutient, and diaphoretic. *d.* half a mifkal to two direms.

(1099) شوكران SHOWKERÁN. Black henbane feed. p. *tokhem bung roomee*. تخمبنكرومي

(1100)

(1100) شوكه SHOWKH. A thiſtle.

ऊंटकटारा h. *oont-ké-tá-rá.*

(1101) شيرخشت SHEERKISHT. A ſpecies of manna, which is collected from a barren tree called *derukt bey chowb*, growing in Khoraſan.

prop. cathartic. *ch.* tranſparent, like gum arabic. *d* 7 to 30 direms.

(1102) شيطرج SHEE-TERUJ. An Indian plant.

चीता: h. *cheetá.* p. *ſhee-tureh.* شيتره

prop. detergent. *ch.* Indian. *d.* one miſkal. *cor.* maſtich. *ſuc.* valerian.

(1103) شيح SHEEH. Wormſeed. p. *dirmeneh.* درمنه

prop. deſtroying worms, and deobſtruent. *ch.* Armenian. *d.* half a direm. *ſuc.* wormwood.

(1104) شيربخشير SHEER-BUCK-SHEER. A yellow root growing in Hindoſtan and Caſhmeer.

हरबी h. *hirbee.*

(1105) شيرخشك SHEER-KHOOSHK. A ſpecies of manna collected from the willow in Khoraſan. p. *beid khiſht.* بيدخشت and *beid angee-been.* بيدانكبين

(1106) شيلم SHYLUM. Tares.

ص

(1107) صابون القاف SÁBOON-UL-KÁF. Soap aſhes.

v. *chowbuck uſhnán.* چوبك اشنان

(1108) صابون SÁ-BOON. Soap.

prop. cauſtic, and detergent. *ch.* old. *ſuc.* lime and ſoap aſhes.

(1109) صبر SYB-IR. Aloes. *vide* 344.

prop. drying; cauſing fleſh to grow; cathartic. *ch.* ſocoterine. *d.* to thirty direms. *cor.* gum arabic, and tragacanth.

(1110) صداء الحديد SUDEED-UL-HEDEED. Iron ruſt.

p. *záfrán áhun.* زعفران آهن

(1111) صدف SUD-UF. Any ſhell.

सीपी h. *ſee-pee.*

prop. drying. *d.* one miſkal, or of lime-water three direms. *cor.* honey and jujubes.

(1112) صدپيوند SUD-PY-WUND. Shepherd's ſtaff.

v. *uſſur ur rá-iy.* عصرالراعي

(1113) صعتر SÁ-TUR. Origanum.

p.

p. *cushneh.* اوشه

(1114) صل SEL. The adder. A snake that will not be enchanted.

(1115) صمغ SUMEGH. Gum in general. गोंद h. *goondh.*

prop. astringent. *ch.* gum arabic.

(1116) صمغ السداب SUMEGH U'S SUDÁB. Gum of rue.

(1117) صمغ المحروث SUMEGH-UL-MEHROOS. Asafœtida.

v. *hilteet.* حلتيت *vide* 305.

(1118) صمغ القتاد SUMEGH UL KUSSÁD. Tragacanth. v. *keseerá* كثيرا

(1119) صمغ عربي SEMUGH ÁREBEE. Gum arabic. *vide* 1115.

(1120) صندل احمر SUNDUL AHMER. Red Sandel wood.

रक्तचंदन h. *ruckut chundun.*

p. *sundul soorkh.* صندل سرخ

(1121) صنوبر كبار SENOBIR KOBÁR. The large pine.

p. *derukht chulghozeh.* درخت چلغوزه

prop. fattening. *ch.* fresh, large, white. *d.* fifteen kernels.

(1122) صنوبر صغار SE-NO-BIR SEGHÁR. The lesser pine.

(1123) صندل ابيض SUNDUL ABIYUZ. White sandel wood.

चंदन h. *chundun.*

p. *sundul sefeid* صندل سفيد

prop. cordial. *d.* half a miskal.

(1124) صوف SOOF. Wool.

ऊन h. *oon.* p. *pushm.* پشم

(1125) صوطله SOOTLEH. A species of beet.

ض

(1126) ضان ZÁN. A sheep.

भेड़ h. *bheir.* p. *meish.* میش

(1127) ضفدع ZUFDTH. A frog.

मेंडुक h. *meidook.* p. *ghowk.* غوک

ط & ظ

(1128) طاؤس TÁOUS. A peacock. मोर h. *moor.*

(1129) طبرزد TUB-IR-ZUD. Sugar candy.

(1130) طباشير TE-BÁ-SHEER. Sugar of bamboo. *vide* 546.

prop. drying, cardiac and tonic. *d.* two dangs in rose water. *suc.* half the weight of camphor.

(1131) طحلب TOHLUB. Water moss.

prop. repellent. *eb.* what grows on sweet water.

(1132) طرفا TURFÁ. The tamarisk tree. *vide* 36.

prop. astringent, and drying. *eb.* that which grows at some distance from water. *d.* five direms. *cor.* oil of almonds and honey.

(1133) طراثيث TERASEE'S. *a.* Name of a fruit. p. *bil.* بل

prop. astringent. *eb.* white. *d.* two miskals. *cor.* tragacanth.

(1134) طرثوث TURSOOS. A thorny tree which produces the gum ammoniac. p. *derukht ushuc.* درخت اشق

(1135) طرخون TURKHOON. *a.* Tarregon, or dranculus hortensis. *vide* 1210.

(1136) طلا TE-LÁ. Gold; also old wine. *vide* 596.

(1137) طلق TULK. Talc. अभ्रक h. *ubhruc.* a. *kokub ul urz.* كوكب الارض

prop. astringent. *cor.* oil and warm water.

(1138) طهف TEHF. A grain. v. *zoorut.* ذرت

(1139) طين احمر TEEN AHMER. Red earth. गेरू h. *geeroo.* p. *gil soorkh.* گل سرخ

(1140) طين شاموش TEEN SHÁ MOOSH. Samian earth.

(1141) طين مختوم TEEN MUKHTOOM. Sealed earth.

prop. astringent, and cordial. *d.* two direms.

(1142) طين TEEN. Earth; bole. मट्टी h. *mittee.* p. *gil.* گل

(1143) طين ارمني TEEN URMENEE. Bole armenic. p. *gil urmenee.* گل ارمني

(114+)

(1144) طين قبرسي TEEN KUB-RUSSEE. Cyprus earth.

(1145) طين فارسي TEEN FARSEE. Persian earth, used for cleansing the head. p. *gil sirshew.* گل سرشوي

(1146) ظبي ZUBBEE. A deer. हिरन h. *hurn.* p. *áhoo.* آهو

(1147) ظفيره ZU-FEERÁH. Wild mint. p. *powdeneh birree.* پودنه بري

(1148) ظلف ZILF. The hoof of any animal. खुर h. *khoor.* p. *soom.* سم

(1149) ظيان ZY-ÁN. Wild jasmin. जाहीजुही *jáhee-jewhee.* p. *yásmeen birree.* ياسمين بري

prop. caustic. *cor.* oil of roses. *suc.* laurel and squills.

ع

(1150) عاقرقرحا AKIR-KER-HÁ. Dranculus.

prop. discutient, and attenuant. *ch.* pungent. *d.* two dangs. *cor.* raisins, or liquorice.

(1151) عاج AWJ. Ivory. हाथीदांत h. *háthee dánt.* p. *den-dán feel.* دندان فيل

prop. drying. *d.* half a direm rasped.

(1152) عبهر UBHIR. The narcissus. p. *nurgis.* نرگس

(1153) عبير A-BEER. Saffron. v. *záfrán.* زعفران

(1154) عتم UT-UM. The wild olive. p. *zietoon kouhee.* زيتون کوهي

(1155) عدس مر UD-US MURR. The bitter pea. p. *musheng telkh.* مشنك تلخ

(1156) عرطنيثا UR-TÁ-NEE-SÁ. Sowbread. *vide* 407, and 543.

(1157) عروق حمرا U-ROOK-HUMRÁ. Madder.

(1158) عرطب URTUB. A small creeping plant. *vide* 790. p. *bussuck.* حسك

(1159) عرعر UR-UR. The mountain pine.

(1160) عروق الصفر U-ROOK-US-SEFR. Turmeric. *vide* 1153.

prop.

prop. discutient, attenuant, and diaphoretic. *ch.* hard. *d.* half a direm.

(1161) عروق U-ROOK. Roots in general. p. *beiykh-há.* بيخها

(1162) عروسك É-ROO-SUC. A small insect, of a beautiful scarlet colour. बीरबहोटी h. *beer-be-bowtee.*

(1163) عروق الصباغين U-ROOK US SE-BÁGHEEN. Turmeric. p. *zirdchowbeh.* زردچوبه

(1164) عروسك در پرده UR-OO-SUC-DIR-PIRDEH. Winter cherry. *vide* 443.

(1165) عزيز UZ-EEZ. Centaury.

(1166) عسل القصب USSUL UL KUSSEB. Juice of the sugar cane. रस h. *russ.* p. *sheereh nei shuckir.* شيره نيشكر

(1167) عسل النحل USSUL-UL-NEHL. Honey. मधु h. *mudhoo.* p. *shehud.* شهد

prop. detergent, and heating. *ch.* of a light yellow, pure, and fragrant.

(1168) عصاره USSA-REH. Expressed juice. p. *ufshoordeh.* افشرده

(1169) عصفر USFIR. Safflower. *vide* 44.

(1170) عصفور US-FOOR. A Sparrow. p. *kunjushk.* كنجشك

(1171) عصي الراعي USSÚR-RAIY. Shepherd's staff. *vide* 61.

(1172) عضاة UZ-UT. General name for thorny plants.

(1173) عضرس IZRISS. Wild mallows. p. *khitmee birree.* خطمي بري

(1174) عضل UZUL. The field mouse. p. *moosh-kuc.* مشكك

(1175) عظم UZM. Bone. हड्डी h. *buddee.* p. *ustukhán.* استخوان

(1176) عظلم IZLUM. The Indigo plant. p *derukht neel.* درخت نيل

(1177) عفص ÚF-ES. Gall apple. माजूफल h. *májoophul.* p. *mazoo.* مازو

prop. astringent and styptic. *ch.* green, not perforated. *d.* half a direm.

(1178) عقرب UKRUB. A scorpion. बिछू h. *beechew.* p. *khezjhem.* كژدم

prop. expelling gravel.

(1179) عقيق UKEEK. A cornelian.

prop. drying. *ch.* those found in Yemen, that

are

are very red and tranſparent. *d.* half a direm. *ſuc.* amber.

(1180) علث ILSS. Wild ſuccory.

p. *káſ-nee birree.* كاسني بري

(1181) عليق U-LIEK. The bramble.

p. *toot-ſeh gúl.* توت سه گل

prop. aſtringent. *d.* of the root three direms. *cor.* liquorice root. *ſuc.* pomegranate buds.

(1182) علك بغدادي UL-UK BÁGHDÁ-DEE. Maſtich.

v. *muſtucká.* مصطكي

(1183) عنب IN-UB. Grápes. *vide* 885.

(1184) عنب الثعلب IN-UB US SÁ-LEB. Fox's grapes, nightſhade.

मकोय *má-ko-ey.*

p. *robá tirbuc.* روباه تربك

prop. repellent. *eb.* yellow, and freſh. *cor.* ſugarcandy, or honey.

(1185) عناب UN-ÁB. Jujubes.

prop. emollient. *d.* in decoction fifteen plums. *ſuc.* raiſins.

(1186) عنكبوت UN-KE-BOOT. A ſpider. मकरी h. *muckree.*

p. *de-yú-pa.* ديوپا

(1187) عنزروت UNZEROOT. Sarcocolla. *vide* 290.

(1188) عنبر UMBIR. Ambergris.

prop. cephalic, and cardiac. *eb.* of an aſh colour.

(1189) عنصل UNSOOL. Squills. *vide* 139.

(1190) عندم UNDUM. Red ſaunders. p. *buckum.* بقم

(1191) عود الصليب OWD US SELEEB. Name of a root. *vide* 1203.

(1192) عود العطاس OWD-UL-UTÁS. ſneezewort. *vide* 209.

(1193) عود الدرقه OWD-UD-DERKEH. Root of the aſafœtida plant.

p. *beikh ungudán.* بيخ انگدان

(1194) عود هندي OWD HINDEE. Lignum aloes. *vide*

prop. deobſtruent, diaphoretic, cephalic, and cardiac. *d.* half a direm.

(1195) عين ÁIN. An eye.

आँख h. *ánkh.* p. *cheſhem.* چشم

غ

(1196) غافث GHÁFIS. Hemp-agrimony.

prop. deobſtruent *eb.* Perſian. *d.* one miſkal.

(1197) غار GHAR. The laurel.

prop. diſcutient and attenuant. *d.* half a miſkal.

(1198) غاسول GHÁSOOL. Glaſſ-wort. *vide* 163.

(1299) غاريقون GHA-REE-KOON. Agaric.

prop. deobſtruent; deſtroying worms; cathartic. *d.* one or two dangs. *ſuc.* as a cathartic turbeth root; and wormſeed againſt worms.

(1200) غرب GHIRB. The mountain pine.

prop. drying. *eb.* the fruit.

(1201) غوره GHOWREH. Every kind of green fruit.

ف

(1202) فاشرا FÁSHERA. Bryony.

p. *kerm deſhty.* كرم‌دشتي

(1203) فاوانيا FÁ-WE-NYÁ. A root.

p. *owd ſelub.* عود‌صليب

prop. aſtringent, deobſtruent, and diaphoretic. *d.* half a miſkal. *cor.* tragacanth. *ſuc.* agaric, and round birthwort.

(1204) فادج FÁDUJ. Bezoar ſtone.

जहर मोहरा: h. *zehr mohrá.* p. *pádzir kánee.* پادزهركاني

(1205) فانيذ FÁ-NEEZ. A kind of barley ſugar. बताशा: h. *be-tá-ſeh.*

(1206) فار FÁR. A rat, or mouſe.

चुहा h. *chewhá.* p. *mooſh.* موش

(1207) فاخته FÁKHTEH. A dove.

पंडुकी h. *pindekee.*

(1208) فجل FUJL. A radiſh.

मूली h. *moolee.* p. *toorb* ترب

(1209) فرنجمشك FERENJ MISHK. A ſpecies of ſweet baſil. तोलसी h. *tulſee.* p. *bálungoo khoord.* بالنكوي‌خورد

(1210) فربيون FIR-BE-YOON, and فرفيون FIR-FE-YOON. Euphorbium.

p. *ſheer derukht zekoom.* شيردرختزقوم

prop. cauſtic, attenuant, and cathartic. *ch.* yellow, and clean.

(1211) فراسيون FE-RÁ-SE-YOON.

Wild leek.

p. *gund-ná-iy koubee.* كندناي كوهي

(1212) فستق FISTOOK. Piſtachio.

p. *piſteh.* پسته

(1213) فضه FIZZEH. Silver.

रूपा h. *roopá.* p. *nockeráh.* نقره

(1214) فطر FETR. Muſhroom.

p. *ſimároogh.* سماروغ

(1215) فطراساليون FETRA-SÁ-LI-YOON. Seed of wild parſley.

tokhem kereſs kouhee. تخم كرفس كوهي

(1216) فلفل اسود FILFIL USWUD.

Black pepper. मिर्च

h. *meeritch* p. *filfil ſee-áh.* فلفل سياه

(1217) فلفل دراز FILFIL DRAJ.

Long pepper. पिलपिल h. *pilpil.*

(1218) فلفل ابيض FILFIL Á-BI-YÚZ. White pepper.

filfil ſepeid. فلفل سپيد

(1219) فلنجمشك FELUNJ MISHK.

The ſame as No. 1209.

(1220) فل FUL. Root of the Indian nelufir.

p. *beikh nelufir hindee.* بيخ نيلوفر هندي

(1221) فلفل مويه FILFIL MOOYEH.

Root of the long pepper buſh.

पीपलामूल h. *peeplámool.* p. *beikh derukht filfil dráz.* بيخ درخت فلفل دراز

(1222) فلفل بري FILFIL BIRREE.

Seed of the agnus caſtus.

(1223) فنطافلون FEN-TA-FE-LOON. Cinquefoil.

p. *punjungooſht.* پنجنكشت

(1224) فوفل FOOFUL. Beetlenut.

सुपारी h. *ſoopáree.*

prop. aſtringent. *d.* half a direm.

(1225) فو FOO. Valerian.

जाललकरी h. *jál-láckree.*

prop. attenuant. *ch.* freſh, fragrant. *d.* half a direm. *ſuc.* aniſeed.

(1226) فوه FOOH. Madder..

(1227)

ق

(1227) قاراسيا KERÁ SYÁ. Cherries. p. *áloo báloo.* آلوبالو

(1228) قاقله KÁKELEH. Cardamoms. *vide* 18.

(1229) قانصه KÁ-NI-SEH. The gizzard of any bird. पथरी h. *puthree.* p. *sungdáneh.* سنگدانه

(1230) قتاد KE-TÁD. The tree which produces gum tragacanth. p. *kum.* کم

(1231) قثا KE-SÁ. A species of long cucumber. ककुरी h. *kuckree.* p. *khyár dráz.* خياردراز

(1232) قثاءالحمار KE-SÁ-UL HY-MÁR. Wild cucumber.

करेला h. *kereylá.*

prop. cathartic and emetic. *d.* of the expressed juice two dáneks. *cor.* tragacanth.

(1233) قت KE-TÁH. A species of clover. v. *ispis.* اسپست

(1234) قردمانا KOOR-DU-MÁ-NÁ. Cardmine.

v. *kur-we-yá jebulee.* كروياجبلي

prop. deobstruent, attenuant, and diaphoretic. *d.* one miskal. *cor.* aniseed. *suc.* mustard seed.

(1235) قرن البحر KERN-UL-BEHR. Amber. p. *kehro-bá.* كهربا

(1236) قرمز KERMEZ. Kermes, used in dying.

(1237) قرع KE-RÁ. A species of gourd. p. *kud-oo.* كدو

(1238) قرنفل KERUNFUL. Cloves. लौंग h. *lowng.* p. *meykuc.* ميخك

(1239) قرون السنبل KEROON US SEMBEL. A poisonous plant, the filaments of which are sometimes found amongst Indian spikenard.

संगियाजहर h. *sun-gee-yá-zehr.*

(1240) قرفةالقرنفل KERFET 'UL KERUNFUL. An aromatic bark, of the colour of cloves.

(1241) قرن KERN. Horn.

सींग h. *seeng.* p. *shákh.* شاخ

(1242) قرطم KOORTEM. Safflower. *vide* 44-450-856.

(1243) قرةالعين KOORUT'L AIN. A kind of water cresses.

p. *kerefs ul máá.* كرفس الما

prop. detergent; and destroying worms. *d.* in decoction five direms.

(1244) قرطم هندي KOORTEM HINDEE. A purgative ſeed. v. *hub ul neel.* حب النيل

(1245) قسط KUST. Coſtus.

(1246) قسط هندي KUST-HINDEE. Bitter coſtus. p. *kuſt telkh.* قسط تلخ

(1247) قشر KISHR. Bark of any tree. छिलका h. *chilká.* p. *poſt.* پوست

(1248) قصب بوا KUSSEB BEWÁ. Calamus aromaticus. *vide* 672.

(1249) قصب KUSSEB. The common reed. p. *nie.* ني

(1250) قصب السكر KUSSEB U'S SOOKIR. Sugar cane. h. ऊंख *ookh.* p. *nie ſhuckir.* نيشكر

(1251) قطونا KUT-OO-NÁ. Fleawort. p. *uſ-pe-ghool.* اسپغول

(1252) قطن KOOTN. Cotton. रुई h. *rewie.* p. *pembeh.* پنبه

(1253) قطران KIT-RÁN. Pitch.

(1254) قلت KOOLT. Saxifrage. v. *káſir ul hejr.* كاسر الحجر

(1255) قلب KULB. The heart. p. *dil.* دل

(1256) قلي KIL-EE. Soap aſhes. साजी h. *ſajee.* v. *kil-ee-yá* قليا

(1257) قنب KINNUB. Hemp. भांग h. *bángh.* p. *báng.* بنك
prop. narcotic, and inebriating.

(1258) قيل KEEL. Pitch. राल h. *rál.* p. *keer.* قير

(1259) قيصوم KYSOOM. Mugwort. v. *bir-un-já-ſif.* برنجاسف

ک .

(1260) كاهربا KÁH-RO-BÁ. Amber.

(1261) كاكنج KÁKE-NUJ. Winter cherry. *vide* 443.
prop. narcotic. *d.* two direms.

(1262) كافور KÁ-FOOR. Camphor.

(1263) كاجر GÁ-JIR. गाजर Carrot.

(1264) كاشم KÁ-SHEM. The aſafœtida plant.

(1265) گاوزبان GÁO-ZEBÁN. p. Bugloſs. a. *liſſán us ſáur.* لسان الثور

(1266) کاهو KÁ-HOO. Lettuce. p. *khuſs.* خس

(1267) کاسني KÁ-SE-NEE. कासनी Endive. p. *hin-de-bá.* هندبا

(1268) کانکني KÁN-GNEE. कांगनी Millet. p. *urzun.* ارزن

(1269) کبريت KIB-REET. Sulphur. गंधक h. *gundhuck.* p. *gowgird.* کوکرد

prop attenuant, and drying. *d.* as far as two direms. *cor.* water melon.

(1270) کبيکج KUB-EE-KUJ. Water creſſes. देवकांडर h. *deo-kán-dur.*

(1271) کبر KUB-IR. Capers.

(1272) کپاس KÉ-PASS. कपास The cotton ſhrub.

p. *derukht pembeh.* درخت پنبه

(1273) کبابه KE-BÁ-BEH. Cubebs.

(1274) کتک KUT-UC. The crab apple. p. *ſeeb birree.* سيب بري

(1275) کتهل KUT-HUL. कटहल An Indian fruit, called by Europeans, *jack*, and which reſembles the hedgehog.

(1276) کتان KUT-ÁN. Linſeed. p. *ulſee.* السي

(1277) کثيرا KE-SEE-RÁ. Gum tragacanth. कठीरा h. *kut,hee-rá.*

prop. allaying thirſt. *d.* half a miſkal. *cor.* aniſeed. *ſuc.* gum arabic.

(1278) کچور KE-CHOOR. कचुर Zerumbád. p. *zerumbád.* زرنباد

(1279) کچنار KUTCH-NÁR. कछनार An Indian tree, bearing purple buds, which the natives boil and eat with bread or rice.

(1280) کجپيپل GUJ-PEEPUL. गजपीपल The fruit of the *cháb* tree. p. *ſemr cháb.* ثمرچاب

(1281) کچلون KUTCHLOON. कचलोन The droſs of glaſs.

p. *nim-uck ſheeſheh.* نمک شيشه

(1282) کحل ROHUL. Antimony. अंजन h. *unjen.* p. *ſoormeh.* سرمه

(1283) کدوي تلخ KUD-EW-EE TELKH. *p.* The bitter gourd. तोंबरी h. *toombree.*

(1284) کدم KUD-UM. कदम An Indian yellow flower, round like a ball.

(1285)

(1285) كرويا KUR-WEE-YÁ. Caraway ſeed.

(1286) كروندا KEROWNDÁ. करौंदा An Indian fruit, reſembling the gooſe-berry.

(1287) كرنب KIR-NUB. Cabbage. p. *ke-lum.* كلم

prop. emollient, and ſuppurative.

(1288) كراث KOORNÁSS. Leeks. *gun-de-ná.* كندنا

(1289) كرفس KEREFS. Parſley. अजमुद h. *ujmood.*

prop. deobſtruent, and diaphoretic. *cb.* garden.

(1290) كرش KOORSH. Tripe. ऊजरी h. *uj-e-ree.* v. *ſhe-kum-beh.* شكنبه

(1291) كرك KIRG. The rhinoceros. गैंडा h. *gyndá.* p. *kur-gud-án.* كركدن

(1292) كرك GOORG. *p.* The wolf. हुनडार h. *hoondár.*

(1293) كرم KERM. The vine. *vide* 194.

(1294) كركم KOORKUM. Saffron.

(1295) كزمازك GUZ-MÁ-ZUC. The fruit of the tamariſk tree.

(1296) كزانكبين GUZ-UNGU-BEEN. A ſpecies of manna collected from the tamariſk tree.

(1297) كسير KU-SEER. Dry pitch. p. *zift kooſhk.* زفت خشك

(1298) كسنبه KU-SUMBH. कुसंभ Safflower. *vide* 450. v. *másfir.* معصفر

(1299) كستوري KUS-TOO-REE. Muſk. p. *mooſhk.* مشك

(1300) كشمش KISHMISH. A ſpecies of raiſins without ſeed. v. *me-weez ungoor beydáneh.* مويزانكوربيدانه

(1301) كشوث رومي KU-SHOOS ROOMEE. Wormwood. *vide* 224.

(1302) كل GOOL. *p.* Any flower. फुल h. *phool.*

(1303) كل GIL. *p.* Earth, clay.

(1304) كلاغ KE-LÁGH. *p.* A crow. v. *zág.* زاغ a. *gherab.* غراب कौवा h. *kow-wá.*

(1305) كلم KE-LUM. *p.* A cabbage.

(1306) كليجن KO-LEE-JUN. Galangal. *vide* 855.

(1307)

(1307) كمافيطوس KE-MÁ-FEE-TOOS. Ground pine.

p. *máshdároo.* ماش دارو

prop. deobstruent, and detergent. *d.* one miskal. *cor.* aniseed.

(1308) كمادريوس KE-MÁ-DREE-YOOS. Germander.

prop. attenuant, deobstruent, and diaphoretic. *d.* one miskal. *cor.* quince. *suc.* agrimony.

(1309) كمرك KUMRUCK. कमरक An Indian fruit.

(1310) كمون KE-MOON. Cumin seed. जीराः h. *zeeráh.*

(1311) كمثري KU-MUS-RÁ. *a.* A pear, *vide* 274.

prop. astringent, and cardiac. *d.* of the juice one wekyàh. *cor.* honey and water. *suc.* quinces.

(1312) كنار KÓ-NÁR. A species of plum. बेर h. *be-ir.*

(1313) كندر KOONDIR. Frankincense.

prop. narcotic. astringent, styptic, cephalic, and cardiac. *ch.* white round grains. *d.* half a direm. *suc* mastich.

(1314) كنير KE-NEER. कनेर Rhododaphne. p. *khurzereh.* خرزهره

(1315) كهربا KEH-RO-BA. Amber.

(1316) كهار KHAR. खार Salt obtained from burnt vegetables; fixed alkaline salt.

(1317) كهيوكوار GHEEKWAR. घीकुवार The aloe plant.

(1318) كهاري لون KÁ-REE-LOON. खारीलोन Sea salt.

p. *nemuck shoor.* نمك شور

(1319) كهنكچي GHOONG-CHEE. घोंगची A red berry used as a weight, and commonly called a *rutty.* *vide* 759.

(1320) كيلا KAY-LA. केला The plantain, the Indian fig. v. *mowz.* موز

(1321) كيسر KEY-SIR. Saffron.

(1322) كيل KEEL. *p.* The medlar. *vide* 622. v. *zá-roos.* زعرور

(1323) كيسو KEY-SOO. An odoriferous grass.

ل

(1324) لاژورد LAZJÉ-WIRD. Lapis lazuli. v. *lajwird.* لجورد

prop. cathartic and cardiac. *ch.* Budakhſhany. *d.* one direm. *cor.* maſtich.

(1325) لادن LÁ-DUN. Labdanum, a reſinous ſubſtance.

prop. attenuant, ſuppurative, diſcutient. *ch.* greaſy, of a yellow tinge. *d.* one direm. *cor.* roſe water and ſandal wood.

(1326) لاغيه LÁ-GHEEYETT. A milky plant, bearing a yellow flower, and whoſe leaves are tinged with the ſame colour. It grows at the foot of mountains.

prop. cauſtic. *ch.* very juicy. *d.* two dangs. *cor.* tragacanth.

(1327) لاكه LÁKH. लाख Stick lac. v. *look.* لك

(1328) لبلاب LUBLÁB. Ivy. v. *aiſhk peitchán.* عشق پيچان

(1329) لبن LEBN. Milk. दूध h. *dood.* p. *ſheir.* شير

(1330) لبان LUBÁN. Olibanum, a ſpecies of frankincenſe. v. *koondir.* كندر

(1331) لحم LEHM. Fleſh. मास h. *máſs.* p. *gowſht.* گوشت

(1332) لحيةالتيس LEHEET-ÚT TEES. Goat's beard, a ſhrub. p. *derukht ſeers.* درخت سرس

prop. aſtringent. *d.* one miſkal to two direms. *cor.* aniſeed.

(1333) لسان الكلب LISSÁN UL KULB. Hound's tongue; cynogloſſum.

(1334) لسان لثور LISSÁN U'S SAUR. Bugloſs. *vide* 6-68.

(1335) لسان الحمل LISSÁN UL HEML. Arnogloſſum. p. *weruck bártung.* ورق بارتنك

(1336) لعبت بربري LÁ-BUT BIRBIRREE. Hermodactyls. *vide* 179-797.

(1337) لفاح LU-FÁH. Fruit of the mandrake.

(1338) لوبيا LOO-BEE-YÁ. A ſpecies of bean.

prop. diaphoretic, and emetic. *ch.* red.

(1339) لوزحلوومر LOUZ HELOU WÙ MURR. Sweet and bitter almonds. p. *bá-dam ſher ſhereen wu telkh.* بادامشيرين وتلخ

prop. The ſweet, provocative, and the bitter, deobſtruent. *ch.* large and oily. *d.* ten direms.

(1340) لوطوس LOOTOOS. Syr. The lotus, or water lily.

कँवल h. *kowul.*

a. *hundkookee.* حندقوقي

p. *neelufir.* نيلوفر

(1341) لوف LOOF. Dragonwort. *vide* 67-183.

prop. deſtroying worms; deobſtruent. *d.* one direm. *cor.* endive. *ſuc.* root of the caper buſh.

(1342) لوبان LOOBAN. Male frankincenſe, of a reddiſh tinge.

v. *koondir zuckir.* كندر ذكر

(1343) لولو LOOLOO. Pearl.

मोती h. *mow-tee.*

p. *mir-wár-reed.* مرواريد

(1344) ليلنج LEE-LUNJ. The Indigo plant. v. *neel.* نيل

(1345) ليمو LEE-MOO. A lemon.

नेंबु h. *neem-boo.*

م

(1346) ماميثا MÁ-MEE-SÁ. A ſpecies of poppy.

(1347) مارماهيج MAR-MÁ-HEEJ. The eel. बामछली h. *bam mutchlee.*

p. *mar-má-hee.* مارماهي

(1348) ماءالشعير MÁ-U'S-SHI-EER. Barley water.

जोवपानी h. *jow pá-nee.*

(1349) ماش MASH. A ſpecies of pea.

मोंग h. *mowng* p. *be-noo-máſh.* بنوماش

(1350) مازريون MÁ-ZIR-YOON. Mezereon root. p. *muſtroo.* مست رو

prop. detergent, and cathartic; the ſeed emetic. *ch.* the plant full of leaves. *d.* half a direm. *cor.* ſteeping it in vinegar.

(1351) ماميران MÁ-MEE-RÁN. A ſpecies of yellow wood.

prop. deobſtruent, and diaphoretic.

(1352) ماهفرنين MAH-FIR-FEEN. Zedoary. p. *judwár.* جدوار

(1353) مارچوبه MAR-CHOO-BEH. Aſparagus. नाकदोन h. *nákdown.*

v. *bil-*

v. *hil-yoon.* هليون p. *margee-ab.* ماركياه

(1354) مازو MAZOO. Gall apple. माजुफल h. *má-joo-phul.* p. *uf-is.* عفص

(1355) ماهودانه MÁHOO-DÁNEH. माहुदाना A seed. v. *hub ul mullook.* حب الملوك

prop. emetic, and cathartic. *d.* one direm.

(1356) ماش هندي MÁSH HINDEE. *p.* Saxifrage. पंवाल h. *punwar.* v. *koolt.* قلت

(1357) متر MUTHUR. मटर Peas. p. *kir-se-neh.* كرسنه

(1358) مثلث MU'-SUL-US. Juice of grapes boiled down to one third.

(1359) مثنان MUS-NÁN. A species of mezereon, which produces the seed called *kirm dá-neh.*

(1360) مجنج MOOJ-NUJ. A plant whose leaves are beautifully variegated. कुलफा h. *kulfa.* p. *khooshnuz-ir* خوش نظر

(1361) مجيته ME-JEETH. मजीठ: Red wood. a. *buckum.* بقم

(1362) محلب MELUB. A tree bearing a berry called *hub mehlub,* and which resembles pear seed.

(1363) محروث MEH-ROOS. Root of the asafœtida plant.

prop. attenuant. *ch.* white, and light.

(1364) مرقشيشا MIR-KÁ-SHEE-SHA. Marcasite. *vide* 82. सोनमाखी h. *soon-mukhee.* v. *hejr u'noor.* حجر النور

prop. astringent.

(1365) مرماحوز MIRMÁ-HOOZ. A species of merow. *vide* 1375.

(1366) مرورشك MIR-WIRUSHK. A species of merow. *vide* 1375.

(1367) مردارسنج MOORDÁRSUNJ. Litharge of lead. p. *moordár-sung.* مردارسنك

(1368) مر MURR. Myrrh. बोल h. *bowl.*

(1369) مرمر MIRMIR. Marble.

(1370) مرزنجوش MIR-ZUN-JOASH. Marjoram.

(1371) مرق ME-RUCK. Broth. p. *shoorbá.* شوربا

(1372) مرجان MER-JÁN. Coral. *vide* 417-484-781.

(1373) مرانيه ME-RÁ-NEE-YEH.

A

A tree reſembling jaſmin. There are two ſpecies; that which is moſt fragrant, or *mirmáhooz*; and another leſs fragrant, called *ſemooſeh* and *mirwiruſhk*. *vide* 1367 and 1368.

(1374) مزمارالراعي MIZMAR UR RÁIY. Shepherd's pipe; called alſo ſhepherd's ſtaff. *vide* 61.

(1375) مس MISS. *p.* Copper. तांबा h. *támbá*. a. *nohâſs*. نحاس

(1376) مسك MISK. Muſk. *vide* 1299. कस्तुरी h. *kuſtowree*. p. *mooſhk*. مشك

(1377) مشمش MISHMISH. Apricot. खुबानी h. *khoobánee*. p. *zirdáloo*. زرد آلو

(1378) مشك الرمان MISHK UR' RÁ MÁN. A beautiful flower tree.

नागेसर h. *nágeyſir*.

(1379) مصطكي MUSTEKÁ Maſtich.

(1380) معصفر MÁSFIR. Safflower. *vide* 44-456-966.

(1381) مغرة MOGHRAH. Red earth.

prop. aſtringent; drying. *ch.* bright red. *d.* half a miſkal. *cor.* honey.

(1382) مغناطيس MIK-NÁ-TEES. The magnet.

चमकपथर h. *chum-uck puthher*. p. *ſung áhun robá*. سنك اهن ربا

(1383) مقل MOKUL. Bdellium. *vide* 222-408-864-908.

(1384) ملح MELH. Salt. लोन h. *loon*. p. *nemuck*. نمك

(1385) ملخ MUL-UC. A Locuſt. टिड्डी h. *tiddee*. a. v. *jé-rád*. جراد

(1386) من MUNN. Manna; general name for all kinds of honey dew. *vide* 611.

(1387) موي كياه MOO-EY GEE-AH. The hairy graſs; Indian ſpikenard. *vide* 150-724-726.

(1388) مورد MOWRID. Myrtle. *vide* 127. v. *áſs*. آس

(1389) موز MOWZ. The plantain, or Indian fig. h. *key-lá*. केला

(1390) موته MOWT'H. A ſmall Indian grain. मोट:

(1391) مومياي MO-MEE-IY. Mummy.

(1392) مهاور MEHÁ-WIR. Tincture of gum lac.

(1393)

(1393) مى MEY. *p.* Wine. मद h. *mud.* a. *khumr.* خمر

(1394) ميندهاسينكي MEYNDEH SINGEE. An Indian milky plant.

ن

(1395) ناخن‌بويا NÁKHUN BÚ-YÁ. Perfumed nails. *vide* 208. नखब h. *nukh.*

(1396) نارنج NÁ-RUNJ. An orange.

(1397) نارجيل NÁR-JEEL. A cocoanut. *vide* 722.

(1398) ناردين NARDEEN. Celtic nard. v. *sembel roomee.* سنبل‌رومي

(1399) ناكدون NÁKDOWN. Asparagus. *vide* 1437.

(1400) ناخن‌ديو NAKHUN-DEO. Perfumed nails. *vide* 1395.

(1401) نانخواه NÁN-KHAH. A species of aniseed.

(1402) نحل NEHL. A bee. p. *mug-us á-sul.* مكس‌عسل

(1403) نخل NUKHEL. The date or palm tree. p. *derukht khurmá.* درخت‌خرما

(1404) نخاله NE-KHÁ-LEH. Chaff. भुसी h. *bhoosee.* p. *se-boos.* سبوس

(1405) نرجس NUR-JISS. The narcissus. p. *nurgis.* نركس

(1406) نسرين NUSSREEN. The China rose; the dog-rose. सेवती h. *sow-tee* v. *wurd cheenee.* ورد‌چيني

(1407) نشاسته NE-SHÁS-TEH. *p.* Starch. a. *lubáb ul kum-eh.* لباب‌القمح

(1408) نطرون NUTROON. A species of borax. जवाखार h. *jewa-khar.* p. *booreh urmenee.* بوره‌ارمني

(1409) نعنع NÁ-NÁ. *a.* Mint. *vide* 559.

(1410) نفط NEFT. *a.* Bitumen.

(1411) نمل NEML. *a.* An ant. चींवटी h. *choontee.* p. *moorcháh.* مورچه

(1412) نمام NE-MAM. Mother of thyme. बर्नान h. *bir-nan.* v. *see-sum-bir.* سيسنبر

(1413)

(1413) نيلج NEE-LUJ. Indigo. v. *uſſáreh neel.* عصارة نيل p. *neeleh.* نيله

(1414) نيلوفر NEELUFIR. The winter lily. कंवल h. *kenowl.*

(1415) نيل NEEL. The Indigo plant.

(1416) نيپال NY-PAL. नैपाल A ſpecies of wormſeed plant.

و

(1417) وج WUJ. Sweet ſcented flag. बच h. *butch.* p. *ug-ir toor-kee.* اكر تركي

(1418) ورد WURD. *a.* The red roſe. p. *gul.* كل

(1419) ورد دفلي WURD DIFLEE. The rhododaphne roſe. कनेरकाफूल h. *káneer-ká-phool.*

(1420) وسمه WUS-MEH. A plant, of which women make a decoction, for dying the eyebrows black. p. *weruck neel.* ورق نيل

ه

(1421) هدل زنكي HU-DUL ZUN-GEE. Turbith root. निसवत h. *nys-wul.*

(1422) هرتال HURTAL. हरताल Yellow orpiment. v. *zirneekh zird.* زرنيخ زرد

(1423) هليلج HE-LEE-LUJ. Yellow myrobalans. हरा h. *hirrá.*

(1424) هلدي HULDEE. हलदी Turmeric. v. *zird-choobeh.* زردچوبه

(1425) هليون HULYOON. Aſparagus. *prop* deobſtruent, and diaphoretic. *ch.* garden. *d.* of the ſeed two direms.

(1426) هندبا HIN-DU-BA. Endive. p. *káſnee.* كاسني

(1427) هيل بوا HEEL BU-YÁ. The leſſer cardamom ſeed. v. *ká-keleh ſe-ghár.* قاقله صغار

(1428) هينك HINGH. हींग Aſafœtida. *vide* 305-798.

(1429) هيضان HE-ZEE-MAN. Horſe raddiſh. p. *toorb birree.* ترب بري

ي

(1430) ياقوت YE-Á-COOT. A ruby.

(1431) یاسمین YE-ÁS-MEEN. Jasmin. चंबेली h. *chumbeylee.*

prop. the flowers attenuant, and cephalic. *ch.* white, fragrant. *cor.* camphor.

(1432) يبروج YEB-ROOJ. Mandrake. *vide* 137-173-621.

(1433) يتوع YE-TUÁ. A general name for all milky plants.

(1434) يخصص YUKH-SÍS. A species of parsley, larger than the common plant.

(1435) يخچه YEKH-CHEH. *p.* Hailstones. ओला h. *owlá.* p. *te-gurg,* تگرگ and *zhá-leb.* ژاله

(1436) يذقه YUZ-KEH. *v.* The dwarf elder. v. *khámá uktee.* خاماءاقطي

(1437) يراميع YE-RÁ-MY-Á. *a.* asparagus. *vide* 1400.

(1438) يشف YESHF. Jasper. p. *sung ye-shem.* سنك يشم

(1439) يقطين YUKTEEN. *a.* A general name for plants having tendrils.

(1440) يلنجوج YE-LUN-JOOJ. Lignum aloes. p. *oud hindee.* عودهندي

(1441) ينبوت YUMBOOT. A species of bean. p. *khirnub nubtee.* خرنوبنبطي

INDEX.

B.

Beid

Buſteetaj-

C.

Choontee

D.

E.

F.

G.

H.

Honey,

I.

J.

K.

L.

M.

M.

Mutha,

N.

O.

P.

Q.

R.

S.

Semrchab,

Spleenwort,

T.

U.

Unfak,

V.

W.

Y.

Z.